William Makepeace Thackeray

A Collection of Letters of Thackeray, 1847-1855

William Makepeace Thackeray

A Collection of Letters of Thackeray, 1847-1855

ISBN/EAN: 9783337134877

Printed in Europe, USA, Canada, Australia, Japan

Cover: Foto ©ninafisch / pixelio.de

More available books at **www.hansebooks.com**

A COLLECTION OF

LETTERS OF THACKERAY

WILLIAM MAKEPEACE THACKERAY.

[Engraved by G. Kruell after the crayon portrait by Samuel Laurence.]

A COLLECTION OF

LETTERS OF THACKERAY

1847-1855

WITH PORTRAITS AND REPRODUCTIONS OF

LETTERS AND DRAWINGS

NEW YORK
CHARLES SCRIBNER'S SONS
MDCCCLXXXVII

COPYRIGHT, 1886, 1887
BY CHARLES SCRIBNER'S SONS

[*All rights reserved*]

PUBLISHERS' NOTE.

※※ In arranging the letters for publication, a simple chronological order has been followed, regardless of their relative importance. In some cases the originals were not dated; and in each of these instances an effort has been made to supply the omission. Often it has been possible to do this with certainty; and in that case the date is printed above the letter in Roman type. Where such certainty could not be reached, conjectural dates are given in italics and enclosed in brackets; but even then they have been so far verified by means of incidents referred to in the letters, or other evidence, that they may be depended upon as fixing very closely the time of the notes to which they are attached. In this final arrangement of the letters, and in some additional annotation, the publishers have enjoyed the privilege of advice and assistance from Mr. James Russell Lowell, who kindly consented, with the cordial approval and thanks of Mrs. Brookfield, to give them this aid.

The publishers are permitted to make public the following letter from Mrs. Ritchie to Mrs. Brookfield:

36a ROSARY GARDENS, HEREFORD SQUARE, S. W.
April 28.

MY DEAR MRS. BROOKFIELD:

I am very glad to hear that you have made a satisfactory arrangement for publishing your selections from my Father's letters. I am of course unable myself by his expressed wish to do anything of the sort. While I am glad to be spared the doubts and difficulties of such a work, I have often felt sorry to think that no one should ever know *more* of him. You know better than anyone what we should like said or unsaid, and what he would have wished; so that I am very glad to think you have undertaken the work, and am always your affectionate

ANNE RITCHIE.

LIST OF ILLUSTRATIONS

THE REPRODUCTIONS, UNLESS OTHERWISE SPECIFIED, ARE MADE FROM
DRAWINGS AND LETTERS IN THE POSSESSION
OF MRS. BROOKFIELD.

WILLIAM MAKEPEACE THACKERAY, . . *Frontispiece*
Engraved by G. Kruell after the portrait by Samuel
Laurence.

	PAGE
Vignette—Drawing by Thackeray of Mrs. Brookfield and her two maids, Turpin and Payne,	5
Passage from a letter to Mr. Brookfield, with drawing, "My Barb is at the Postern,"	9
Passage from a letter from Brussels, with drawing, "The Broken Knife,"	10
——From the same letter, with drawing, "The Slashers,"	12
Drawing by Thackeray in water color and pencil (Mrs. Brookfield),	18
Clevedon Court (from a recent photograph),	28
Passage from a letter to Mr. Brookfield, with drawing, "Harry Hallam with Dog and Gun,"	29

	PAGE
Passage from a letter of November 1, 1848, with drawing, "A Party of Us Drove in an Oxford Cart,"	31
——From the same, with drawing, "The Oxford Man's Bed,"	32
Drawing by Thackeray, an equestrian statue of himself,	40
Fac-simile of a minute dinner-note from Thackeray,	51
Sketch of Mrs. Brookfield (from a collection of Thackeray's drawings privately printed for Sir Arthur Elton, of Clevedon Court),	54
In the Nursery at Clevedon Court (from the Clevedon drawings),	62
Passage from a letter from Brighton, with drawing, "An Evening Reading,"	63
Clevedon Church (from a recent photograph),	68
Note sent by Thackeray to Mrs. Elliot, written in the form of the initials J. O. B.,	72
Fac-simile of a letter from Paris, with sketch of Jules Janin,	80
Stanza from the original manuscript of Clough's "Flags of Piccadilly," with a drawing by Thackeray, in the possession of Mr. James Russell Lowell,	82
Note and sketch sent by Thackeray to Mrs. Elliot, in the possession of Miss Kate Perry,	94
Fac-simile of letter from Dieppe, with drawings of Angelina Henrion and a clergyman's wife,	110

	PAGE
"The Lady of the House," a drawing by Thackeray (perhaps Lady Castlereagh?),	114
The Statuette of Thackeray by Joseph Edgar Boehm, R.A.,	118
Memorial Tablets to Arthur and Henry Hallam in Clevedon Church (from a photograph),	130
Sketch by Thackeray,	138
Fac-simile of a letter to Mrs. Elliot, now in the possession of her sister, Miss Kate Perry,	142
In the School-room of Clevedon Court (from the Clevedon drawings),	148
Passage from a letter from Switzerland, with drawing of the View from a Window at Basel,	150
Sketch by Thackeray—His Daughters and Major and Mrs. Carmichael Smyth,	154
Portrait of Thackeray (from a photograph in the possession of Mrs. James T. Fields),	158
Vignette—Profile of the Boehm Statuette,	176
Portrait of Thackeray (from a drawing by Samuel Laurence),	178
Vignette—Drawing sent to Miss Kate Perry,	183

INTRODUCTION.

NO writer of recent times is so much quoted as Thackeray; scarcely a week passes without his name recurring in one or other of the leading articles of the day; and yet whilst his published works retain their influence so firmly, the personal impression of his life and conversation becomes more and more shadowy and indistinct as the friends who knew and loved him the most are gradually becoming fewer and passing away.

Thackeray's nature was essentially modest and retiring. More than once it appears that he had desired his daughter to publish no memoir of him. Mrs. Ritchie, who alone could do justice to her Father's memory, and who has inherited the true woman's share of his genius, and of the tender and perceptive sympathy of his character, has ever held this injunction sacred, even to the extent of withholding all his letters to his family from publication. Yet it happens from time to time that some chance letters of doubtful authenticity, and others utterly spurious, have appeared in print, and have even perhaps found acceptance amongst those who, knowing him only by his published works, were without the true key for distinguishing what was genuine from what was simply counterfeit.

The letters which form this collection were most of them written by Mr. Thackeray to my husband, the late Rev'd W. H. Brookfield, and myself, from about 1847, and continuing during many years of intimate friendship, beginning from the time when he first lived in London, and when he especially needed our sympathy. His happy married life had been broken up by the malady which fell upon his young wife after the birth of her youngest child; his two remaining little girls were under his mother's care, at Paris. Mr. Thackeray was living alone in London. "Vanity Fair" was not yet written when these letters begin. His fame was not yet established in the world at large; but amongst his close personal friends, an undoubting belief in his genius had already become strongly rooted. No one earlier than my dear gifted husband adopted and proclaimed this new faith. The letters now so informally collected together are not a consecutive series; but they have always been carefully preserved with sincere affection by those to whom they were written. Some of them are here given without the omission of a word; others are extracts from communications of a more private character; but if every one of these letters from Thackeray could be rightly made public, without the slightest restriction, they would all the more redound to his honour.

JANE OCTAVIA BROOKFIELD.

29 CARLYLE SQUARE, CHELSEA.

LETTERS.

[*Jan.* 1847.]

[*To Mr. Brookfield.*]

MY DEAR W.:

There will be no dinner at Greenwich on Monday. Dickens has chosen that day for a reconciliation banquet between Forster and me.

Is madame gone and is she better? My heart follows her respectfully to Devonshire and the dismal scenes of my youth.

I am being brought to bed of my seventh darling with inexpressible throes: and dine out every day until *Juice* knows when.

I will come to you on Sunday night if you like—though stop, why shouldn't you, after church, come and sleep out here in the country?

Yours,

JOS. OSBORN.

[*August*, 1847.]

[*To Mr. Brookfield.*]

LE DIMANCHE.

MONSIEUR L'ABBÉ:

De retour de Gravesend j'ai trouvé chez moi un billet de M. Crowe, qui m'invite à diner demain à 6 heures précises à Ampstead.

En même temps M. Crowe m'a envoyé une lettre pour vous,—ne vous trouvant pas à votre ancien logement (où l'adresse de l'horrible bouge où vous demeurez actuellement est heureusement ignorée)—force fut à M. Crowe de s'adresser à moi—à moi qui connais l'ignoble caveau que vous occupez indignement, sous les dalles humides d'une église déserte, dans le voisinage fétide de fourmillants Irlandais.

Cette lettre, Monsieur, dont je parle—cette lettre—je l'ai laissée à la maison. Demain il sera trop tard de vous faire part de l'aimable invitation de notre ami commun.

Je remplis enfin mon devoir envers M. Crowe en vous faisant savoir ses intentions hospitalières à votre égard. Et je vous quitte, Monsieur, en vous donnant les assurances réitérées de ma haute considération.

CHEVALIER DE TITMARSH.

J'offre à Madame l'Abbesse mes hommages respectueux.

1847.

[*To Mr. Brookfield.*]

MY DEAR OLD B.:

Can you come and dine on Thursday at six? I shall be at home—no party—nothing—only me. And about your night-cap, why not come out for a day or two, though the rooms are very comfortable in the Church vaults.* Farewell.

Ever your
LOUISA.

(And Madam, is she well?)

[1847.]

[*Enclosing the following note.*]

TEMPLE, 8 Nov.

MY DEAR THACKERAY:

A thousand thanks. It will do admirably, and I will not tax you again in the same manner. Don't get nervous or think about criticism, or trouble yourself about the opinions of friends; you have completely beaten Dickens out of the inner circle already. I dine at Gore House to-day; look in if you can.

Ever yours,
A. H.

MADAM:

Although I am certainly committing a breach of confidence, I venture to offer my friend up to you, because you have considerable humour, and I think will possibly laugh at

---

* In this Letter, and elsewhere, reference is made to my husband's living in the "church vaults." Our income at this time was very small, and a long illness had involved us in some difficulty. Mr. Brookfield's aversion to debt and his firm rectitude of principle decided him to give up our lodgings, and to remove by himself into the vestry of his District Church, which was situated in a very squalid neighborhood. Here he could live rent free, and in the midst of his parish work, whilst he sent me to stay with my dear father, the late Sir Charles Elton, at Clevedon Court, for the recovery of my health. At this juncture our circumstances gradually brightened. Mr. Thackeray, my uncle, Mr. Hallam, and other friends interested themselves towards obtaining better preferment for Mr. Brookfield, whose great ability and high character were brought to the notice of Lord Lansdowne, then President of the Council, and head of the Education Department. He appointed Mr. Brookfield to be one of H. M. Inspectors of Schools, an employment which was very congenial to him. Our difficulties were then removed, and we were able to establish ourselves in a comfortable house in Portman Street, to which so many of these letters are addressed.

him. You know you yourself often hand over some folks to some other folks, and deserve to be treated as you treat others.

The circumstances arose of a letter which H—— sent me, containing prodigious compliments. I answered that these praises from all quarters frightened me rather than elated me, and sent him a drawing for a lady's album, with a caution not to ask for any more, hence the reply. Ah! Madame, how much richer truth is than fiction, and how great that phrase about the "inner circle" is.

I write from the place from which I heard your little voice last night, I mean this morning, at who knows how much o'clock. I wonder whether you will laugh as much as I do; my papa in the next room must think me insane, but I am not, and am of Madame, the *Serviteur* and *Frère affectionné*.

W. M. T.

[1847.]

[*To Mr. Brookfield.*]

My dear W. H. B.:

I daresay you are disgusted at my not coming to the *bouge*, on Sunday night, but there was a good reason, which may be explained if required hereafter. And I had made up my account for some days at Southampton, hoping to start this day, but there is another good reason for staying at home. Poor old grandmother's will, burial &c., detained me in town. Did you see her death in the paper?

Why I write now, is to beg, and implore, and intreat that you and Mrs. Brookfield will come and take these three nice little rooms here, and stop with me until you have found other lodgment. It will be the very greatest comfort and kindness to me, and I shall take it quite *hangry* if you don't come. Will you come on Saturday now? the good things you shall have for dinner are quite incredible. I have got a box of preserved apricots from Fortnum and Mason's which alone ought to make any lady happy, and two shall be put under my lady's pillow every night. Now do come—and farewell. My barb is at the postern. I have had him clipped and his effect in the Park is quite *tremenjus*.

BRUSSELS, Friday [28 July], 1848.

I have just had a dreadful omen. Somebody gave me a paper-knife with a mother of pearl blade and a beautiful Silver handle. Annie recognised it in a minute, lying upon my dressing table, with a "Here's Mrs. So and So's butter knife." I suppose she cannot have seen it above twice, but that child remembers everything. Well, this morning, being fairly on my travels, and having the butter knife in my desk.

I thought I would begin to cut open a book I had bought, never having as yet had occasion to use it. The moment I tried, the blade broke away from the beautiful handle. What does this portend? It is now—[here drawing] There is a blade and there is a hilt, but they refuse to act together. Something is going to happen I am sure.

I took leave of my family on Sunday, after a day in the rain at Hampton Court. . . . Forster * was dining with Mr. Chapman the publisher, where we passed the day. His article in the *Examiner* did not please me so much as his genuine good nature in insisting upon walking with Annie at night, and holding an umbrella over her through the pouring rain. Did you read the *Spectator's* sarcastic notice of V. F.? I don't think it is just, but think *Kintoul* is a very honest man and rather inclined to deal severely with his private friends, lest he should fall into the other extreme;—to be sure he keeps out of it, I mean the other extreme, very well.

I passed Monday night and part of Tuesday in the artless society of some officers of the 21st, or Royal Scots Fusiliers, in garrison at Canterbury. We went to a barrack room, where we drank about, out of a Silver cup and a glass. I heard such stale old garrison stories. I recognised among the stories many old friends of my youth, very pleasant to meet when one was eighteen, but of whom one is rather shy now. Not so these officers, however; they tell each other the stalest and wickedest old Joe Millers; the jolly grey-headed old majors have no reverence for the beardless en-

---

* John Forster, the intimate friend of Charles Dickens, and well-known writer.

signs, nor *vice-versa*. I heard of the father and son in the other regiment in garrison at Canterbury, the Slashers if you please, being carried up drunk to bed the night before. Fancy what a life. Some of ours,—I don't mean yours Madam, but I mean mine and others—are not much better, though more civilised.

We went to see the wizard Jacobs at the theatre, he came up in the midst of the entertainment, and spoke across the box to the young officers ;—he knows them in private life, they think him a good fellow. He came up and asked them confidentially, if they didn't like a trick he had just performed. " Neat little thing isn't it?" the great Jacobs said, "I brought it over from Paris." They go to his entertainment every night, fancy what a career of pleasure!

A wholesome young Squire with a large brown face and a short waistcoat, came up to us and said, " Sorry you're goin', I have sent up to barracks a great lot o' *rabbuts*." They were of no use, those *rabbuts ;* the 21st was to march the next day. I saw the men walking about on the last day, taking leave of their sweethearts, (who will probably be consoled by the Slashers).

I was carried off by my brother-in-law through the rain, to see a great sight, the regimental soup-tureens and dishcovers, before they were put away. "Feel *that*" says he, "William, just feel the weight of that!" I was called upon twice to try the weight of that soup dish, and expressed the very highest gratification at being admitted to that privilege. Poor simple young fellows and old youngsters! I felt ashamed of myself for spying out their follies and fled from them and came off to Dover. It was pouring with rain all day, and I had no opportunity of putting anything into the beautiful new sketch books.

I passed an hour in the Cathedral, which seemed all beautiful to me; the fifteenth Century part, the thirteenth century part, and the crypt above all, which they say is older than the Conquest. The most charming, harmonious, powerful combination of shafts and arches, beautiful whichever way you saw them developed, like a fine music or the figures in a Kaleidoscope, rolling out mysteriously, a beautiful foundation for a beautiful building. I thought how some people's tower-

a great lot o' rabbits. they were of no use those rabbits, the 21st were to march the next day. I saw the men walking about on the last day taking leave of their sweethearts (who will probably be consoled by the Slashers) I was carried off by my brother in law through the Town to see a great sight - the regimental Soup tureens and dish covers before they were put away. "Feel that" says he, William "Just feel the weight of that." I was called upon twice to try the weight of that Soup dish and expressed the very highest grade pleasure at being admitted to that privilege. Poor simple young fellows and old young men! I felt ashamed of myself for ~~walking about~~ spying and their follies: and fled from them and came off to Canterbury tower.

ing intellects and splendid cultivated geniuses rise upon simple, beautiful foundations hidden out of sight, and how this might be a good simile, if I knew of any very good and wise man just now. But I don't know of many, do you?

Part of the Crypt was given up to French Calvinists; and texts from the French Bible of some later sect are still painted on the pillars, surrounded by French ornaments, looking very queer and out of place. So, for the matter of that, do we look queer and out of place in that grand soaring artificial building: we may put a shovel hat on the pinnacle of the steeple, as Omar did a crescent on the peak of the church at Jerusalem; but it does not belong to us, I mean according to the fitness of things. We ought to go to church in a very strong, elegant, beautifully neat room; croziers, and banners, incense, and jimcracks, grand processions of priests and monks (with an inquisition in the distance), and lies, avarice, tyranny, torture, all sorts of horrible and unnatural oppressions and falsehoods kept out of sight; such a place as this ought to belong to the old religion. How somebody of my acquaintance would like to walk into a beautiful calm confessional and go and kiss the rood or the pavement of a'Becket's shrine. Fancy the church quite full; the altar lined with pontifical gentlemen bobbing up and down; the dear little boys in white and red flinging about the incense pots; the music roaring out from the organs; all the monks and clergy in their stalls, and the archbishop on his throne—O! how fine! And then think of the ✚ of our Lord speaking quite simply to simple Syrian people, a child or two maybe at his knees, as he taught them that love was the truth. Ah! as one thinks of it, how grand that figure looks, and how small all the rest; but I dare say I am getting out of my depth.

I came on hither [to Brussels] yesterday, having passed the day previous at Dover, where it rained incessantly, and where I only had the courage to write the first sentence of this letter, being utterly cast down and more under the influence of blue devils than I ever remember before; but a fine bright sky at five o'clock in the morning, and a jolly brisk breeze, and the ship cutting through the water at fifteen miles an hour, restored cheerfulness to this wearied spirit, and enabled it to partake freely of beefsteak and *pommes-de-terre* at

Ostend; after an hour of which amusement, it was time to take the train and come on to Brussels. The country is delightfully well cultivated; all along the line you pass by the most cheerful landscapes with old cities, gardens, cornfields and rustic labour.

At the *table d'hôte* I sat next a French Gentleman and his lady. She first sent away the bread; she then said "*mais, mon ami, ce potage est abominable;* then she took a piece of pudding on her fork, not to eat, but to smell, after which she sent it away. Experience told me it was a little *grisette* giving herself airs, so I complimented the waiter on the bread, recommended the soup to a man, and took two portions of the pudding, under her nose.

Then we went (I found a companion, an ardent admirer, in the person of a Manchester merchant) to the play, to see Dejazet, in the " *Gentil Bernard*," of which piece I shall say nothing, but I think it was the wickedest I ever saw, and one of the pleasantest, adorably funny and naughty. As the part (*Gentil Bernard* is a prodigious rake,) is acted by a woman, the reality is taken from it, and one can bear to listen, but such a little rake, such charming impudence, such little songs, such little dresses! She looked as *mignonne* as a china image, and danced, fought, sang and capered, in a way that would have sent Walpole mad could he have seen her.

And now writing has made me hungry, and if you please I will go and breakfast at a Café with lots of newspapers, and garçons bawling out " *Voilà M'sieu*"—how pleasant to think of! The Manchester admirer goes to London to-day and will take this. If you want any more please send me word *Poste Restante* at Spa.

I am going to-day to the Hôtel de la Terrasse, where Becky used to live, and shall pass by Captain Osborn's lodgings, where I recollect meeting him and his little wife—who has married again somebody told me;—but it is always the way with these *grandes passions*—Mrs. Dobbins, or some such name, she is now; always an over-rated woman, I thought. How curious it is! I believe perfectly in all those people, and feel quite an interest in the Inn in which they lived.

Good bye, my dear gentleman and lady, and let me hear the latter is getting well.

W. M. T.

HÔTEL DES PAYS BAS, SPA.
August 1st to 5th. 1848.

MY DEAR FRIENDS:

Whoever you may be who receive these lines,—for unless I receive a letter from the person whom I privately mean, I shall send them post-paid to somebody else,—I have the pleasure to inform you, that on yesterday, the 30th, at 7 A.M., I left Brussels, with which I was much pleased, and not a little tired, and arrived quite safe per railroad and *diligence* at the watering place of Spa. I slept a great deal in the coach, having bought a book at Brussels to amuse me, and having for companions, three clergymen (of the deplorable Romish faith) with large idolatrous three-cornered hats, who read their breviaries all the time I was awake, and I have no doubt gave utterance to their damnable Popish opinions when the stranger's ears were closed; and lucky for the priests that I was so situated, for speaking their language a great deal better than they do themselves (being not only image-worshippers but Belgians, whose jargon is as abominable as their superstition) I would have engaged them in a controversy, in which I daresay they would have been utterly confounded by one who had the Thirty-nine Articles of truth on his side. Their hats could hardly get out of the coach door when they quitted the carriage, and one of them, when he took off his, to make a parting salute to the company, quite extinguished a little passenger.

We arrived at Spa at two o'clock, and being driven on the top of the *diligence* to two of the principal hotels, they would not take me in as I had only a little portmanteau, or at least only would offer me a servant's bedroom. These miserable miscreants did not see by my appearance that I was not a flunkey, but on the contrary, a great and popular author; and I intend to have two fine pictures painted when I return to England, of the landlord of the Hôtel d'Orange refusing a bed-chamber to the celebrated Titmarsh, and of the proprietor of the Hôtel d'York, offering Jeames a second-floor back closet. Poor misguided people! It was on the 30th July 1848. The first thing I did after *at length* securing a *handsome* apartment at the Hôtel des Pays Bas, was to survey the town and partake of a glass of water at the Pouhon well, where the late Peter the Great, the imperator of the Bo-Russians appears also to have drunk; so that two great men at least have refreshed themselves at that fountain. I was next conducted to the baths, where a splendid concert of wind and stringed instruments was performed under my window, and many hundreds of gentle-folks of all nations were congregated in the public walk, no doubt to celebrate my arrival. They are so polite however at this place of elegant ease, that they didn't take the least notice of the Illustrious Stranger, but allowed him to walk about quite unmolested and, (to all appearance) unremarked. I went to the *table d'hôte* with perfect affability, just like an ordinary person; an *ordinary* person at the *table d'hôte*, mark the pleasantry. If that joke doesn't make your sides ache, what, my dear friend, can move you? We had a number of good things, fifteen or sixteen too many I should say. I was myself obliged to give in at about the twenty-fifth dish; but there was a Flemish lady near me, a fair blue-eyed being, who carried on long after the English author's meal was concluded, and who said at dinner to-day, (when she beat me by at least treble the amount of victuals) that she was languid and tired all day, and an invalid, so weak and delicate that she could not walk. "No wonder," thought an observer of human nature, who saw her eating a second supply of lobster salad, which she introduced with her knife, " no wonder, my blue-eyed female, that you are ill, when you take such a preposterous quantity of nourishment;" but as the waters of this place are eminently ferruginous, I presume that she used the knife in question for the purpose of taking steel with her dinner. The subject I feel is growing painful, and we will, if you please, turn to more delicate themes.

I retired to my apartment at seven, with the same book which I had purchased, and which sent me into a second sleep until ten when it was time to go to rest. At eight I was up and stirring, at 8.30 I was climbing the brow of a little mountain which overlooks this pretty town, and whence, from among firs and oaks, I could look down upon the spires of the church, and the roofs of the Redoute, and the principal and inferior buildings and the vast plains, and hills beyond, topped in many places with pine woods, and covered with green crops and yellow corn. Had I a friend to walk hand in hand with, him or her, on these quiet hills, the promenade methinks might be pleasant. I thought of many such as I paced among the rocks and shrubberies. Breakfast succeeded that solitary, but healthy reverie, when coffee and eggs were served to the Victim of Sentiment. Sketch-book in hand, the individual last alluded to set forth in quest of objects suitable for his pencil. But it is more respectful to Nature to look at her and gaze with pleasure, rather than to sit down with pert assurance, and begin to take her portrait. A man who persists in sketching, is like one who insists on singing during the performance of an opera. What business has he to be trying his stupid voice? He is not there to imitate, but to admire to the best of his power. Thrice the rain came down and drove me away from my foolish endeavours, as I was making the most abominable caricatures of pretty, quaint cottages, shaded by huge ancient trees.

In the evening was a fine music at the Redoute, which being concluded, those who had a mind were free to repair to a magnificent neighbouring saloon, superbly lighted, where a great number of persons were assembled amusing themselves, round two tables covered with green cloth and ornamented with a great deal of money. They were engaged at a game which seems very simple; one side of the table is marked red and the other black, and you have but to decide which of the red or the black you prefer, and if the colour you choose is turned up on the cards, which a gentleman deals, another gentleman opposite to him gives you five franks, or a napoleon or whatever sum of money you have thought fit to bet upon your favourite colour.

But if your colour loses, then he takes your napoleon. This he did, I am sorry to say, to me twice, and as I thought this was enough, I came home and wrote a letter, full of nonsense to—

[*August* 11th]

MY DEAR MRS. BROOKFIELD :

You see how nearly you were missing this delightful letter, for upon my word I had packed it up small and was going to send it off in a rage to somebody else, this very day, to a young lady whom some people think over-rated very likely, or to some deserving person, when, *O gioja e felicità* (I don't know whether that is the way to spell *gioja*, but rather pique myself on the g) when O! *bonheur suprême*, the waiter enters my door at 10 o'clock this morning, just as I had finished writing page seven of PENDENNIS, and brings me the *Times* newspaper and a beautiful thick 2/4 letter, in a fine large hand. I eagerly seized—the newspaper, (ha ha ! I

[Drawing by Thackeray in water-colour and pencil (Mrs. Brookfield).]

had somebody there) and was quickly absorbed in its contents. The news from Ireland is of great interest and importance, and we may indeed return thanks that the deplorable revolution and rebellion, which everybody anticipated in that country, has been averted in so singular, I may say unprecedented a manner. How pitiful is the figure cut by Mr. Smith O'Brien, and indeed by Popery altogether! &c. &c.

One day is passed away here very like its defunct predecessor. I have not lost any more money at the odious gambling table, but go and watch the players there with a great deal of interest. There are ladies playing—young and pretty ones too. One is very like a lady I used to know, a curate's wife in a street off Golden Square, *whatdyoucallit* street, where the pianoforte maker lives; and I daresay this person is puzzled why I always go and stare at her so. She has her whole soul in the pastime, puts out her five-franc pieces in the most timid way, and watches them disappear under the *croupier's* rake with eyes so uncommonly sad and tender, that I feel inclined to go up to her and say " Madam, you are exceedingly like a lady, a curate's wife whom I once knew, in England, and as I take an interest in you, I wish you would get out of this place as quick as you can, and take your beautiful eyes off the black and red." But I suppose it would be thought rude if I were to make any such statement and— Ah! what do I remember? There's no use in sending off this letter to-day, this is Friday, and it cannot be delivered on Sunday in a Protestant metropolis. There was no use in hurrying home from Lady ———, (Never mind, it is only an Irish baronet's wife, who tries to disguise her Limerick brogue, but the fact is she has an exceedingly pretty daughter), I say there was no use in hurrying home so as to get this off by the post.

Yesterday I didn't know a soul in this place, but got in the course of the day a neat note from a lady who had the delight of an introduction to me at D-v-nsh-re House, and who proposed tea in the most flattering manner. Now, I know a French duke and duchess, and at least six of the most genteel persons in Spa, and some of us are going out riding in a few minutes, the rain having cleared off, the sky being bright, and the surrounding hills and woods looking uncommonly green and tempting.

. . . . . .

A pause of two hours is supposed to have taken place since the above was written. A gentleman enters, as if from horseback, into the room No. 32 of the Hotel des Pays Bas, looking on to the fountain in the Grande Place. He divests himself of a part of his dress, which has been spattered with mud during an arduous but delightful ride over commons, roads, woods, nay, mountains. He curls his hair in the most killing manner, and prepares to go out to dinner. The purple shadows are falling on the Grande Place, and the roofs of the houses looking westward are in a flame. The clock of the old church strikes six. It is the appointed hour; he gives one last glance at the looking-glass, and his last thought is for—(see page 4—last three words.)

The dinner was exceedingly stupid, I very nearly fell asleep by the side of the lady of the house. It was all over by nine o'clock, half an hour before Payne comes to fetch you to bed, and I went to the gambling house and lost two napoleons more. May this be a warning to all dissipated middle-aged persons. I have just got two new novels from the library by Mr. Fielding; the one is *Amelia*, the most delightful portrait of a woman that surely ever was painted; the other is *Joseph Andrews*, which gives me no particular pleasure, for it is both coarse and careless, and the author makes an absurd brag of his twopenny learning, upon which he values himself evidently more than upon the best of his own qualities. Good night, you see I am writing to you as if I was talking. It is but ten o'clock, and yet it seems quite time here to go to bed. . . .

I have got a letter from Annie, so clever, humourous and wise, that it is fit to be printed in a book. As for Miss Jingleby, I admire her pretty face and manners more than her singing, which is very nice, and just what a lady's should be, but I believe my heart is not engaged in that quarter. Why there is six times as much writing in my letter as in yours! you ought to send me ever so many pages if bargains were equal between the male and female, but they never are. There is a prince here who is seventy-two years of age and wears frills to his trowsers.

What if I were to pay my bill and go off this minute to the Rhine? It would be better to see that than these genteel dandies here. I don't care about the beauties of the Rhine any more, but it is always pleasant and friendly. There is no reason why I should not sleep at Bonn to-night, looking out on the Rhine opposite Drachenfels—that is the best way of travelling surely, never to know where you are going until the moment and fate say "go." Who knows? By setting off at twelve o'clock, something may happen to alter the whole course of my life? perhaps I may meet with some beautiful creature who . . . But then it is such a bore, packing up those shirts. I wonder whether anybody will write to me *poste restante* at Homburg, near Frankfort-on-the-Maine? And if you would kindly send a line to Annie at Captain Alexander's, Montpellier Road, Twickenham, telling her to write to me there and not at Brussels, you would add, Madame, to the many obligations you have already conferred on

Your most faithful servant,

W. M. THACKERAY.

I have made a dreadful dumpy little letter, but an envelope would cost 1/2 more. I don't like to say anything disrespectful of Dover, as you are going there, but it seemed awfully stupid. May I come and see you as I pass through? A line at the Ship for me would not fail to bring me.

21 August. [1848] Home.

[*To Mr. Brookfield.*]

MY DEAR OLD B. :

I am just come back and execute my first vow, which was to tell you on landing that there is a certain bath near Minden, and six hours from Cologne by the railway (so that people may go all the way at their ease) where all sorts of complaints —including of course yours, all and several, are to be cured. The bath is Rehda, station Rehda. Dr. Sutro of the London German Hospital, knows all about it. I met an acquaintance just come thence, (a Mrs. Bracebridge and her *mari*) who told me of it. People are ground young there—a young physician has been cured of far gone tubercles in the lungs; maladies of languor, rheumatism, liver complaints, all sorts of wonders are performed there, especially female wonders.

Y not take Madame there, go, drink, bathe, and be cured? Y not go there as well as anywhere else this summer season? Y not come up and see this German doctor, or ask Bullar to write to him? Do, my dear old fellow; and I will vow a candle to honest Horne's chapel if you are cured. Did the Vienna beer in which I drank your health, not do you any good? God bless you, my dear Brookfield, and believe that I am always affectionately yours,

W. M. T.

[1848.]

My dear Mrs. Brookfield:

Now that it is over and irremediable I am thinking with a sort of horror of a bad joke in the last number of *Vanity Fair*, which may perhaps annoy some body whom I wouldn't wish to displease. Amelia is represented as having a lady's maid, and the lady's maid's name is Payne. I laughed when I wrote it, and thought that it was good fun, but now, who knows whether you and Payne and everybody won't be angry, and in fine, I am in a great tremor. The only way will be, for you I fear to change Payne's name to her Christian one. Pray don't be angry if you are, and forgive me if I have offended. You know you are only a piece of Amelia, my mother is another half, my poor little wife—*y est pour beaucoup*.

and I am
Yours most sincerely
W. M. Thackeray.

I hope you will write to say that you forgive me.

October 1848.

13 Young Street, Kensington.

My Dear Lady Brookfield:

I wrote you a letter three nights ago in the French language, describing my disappointment at not having received any news of you. Those which I had from Mrs. Turpin were not good, and it would have been a pleasure to your humble servant to have had a line. Mr. William dined with the children good-naturedly on Sunday, when I was yet away at Brighton.

My parents are not come yet, the old gentleman having

had an attack of illness to which he is subject; but they promised to be with me on Tuesday, some day next week I hope. I virtuously refused three invitations by this day's post, and keep myself in readiness to pass the first two or three evenings on my Papa's lap.

That night I wrote to you the French letter, I wrote one to Miss Brandauer, the governess, warning her off. I didn't send either. I have a great mind to send yours though, it is rather funny, though I daresay with plenty of mistakes, and written by quite a different man, to the Englishman who is yours respectfully. A language I am sure would change a man; so does a handwriting. I am sure if I wrote to you in this hand, and adopted it for a continuance, my disposition and sentiments would alter and all my views of life. I tried to copy, not now but the other day, a letter Miss Procter showed me from her uncle, in a commercial hand, and found myself after three pages quite an honest, regular, stupid, commercial man; such is sensibility and the mimetic faculty in some singularly organized beings. How many people are you? You are Dr. Packman's Mrs. B, and Mrs. Jackson's Mrs. B, and Ah! you are my Mrs. B. you know you are now, and quite different to us all, and you are your sister's Mrs. B. and Miss Wynne's, and you make gentle fun of us all round to your private B. and offer us up to make him sport. You see I am making you out to be an Ogre's wife, and poor William the Ogre, to whom you serve us up cooked for dinner. Well, stick a knife into me, here is my *busam ;* I won't cry out, you poor Ogre's wife, I know you are good natured and soft-hearted *au fond*.

I have been re-reading the *Hoggarty Diamond* this morning; upon my word and honour, if it doesn't make you cry, I shall have a mean opinion of you. It was written at a time of great affliction, when my heart was very soft and humble. Amen. *Ich habe auch viel geliebt.*

Why shouldn't I start off this instant for the G. W. Station and come and shake hands, and ask your family for some dinner; I should like it very much. Well, I am looking out of the window to see if the rain will stop, or give me an excuse for not going to Hatton to the Chief Baron's. I won't go—that's a comfort.

I am writing to William to ask him to come and dine tomorrow, we will drink your health if he comes. I should like to take another sheet and go on tittle-tattling, it drops off almost as fast as talking. I fancy you lying on the sofa, and the boy outside, walking up and down the oss. But I wont. To-morrow is Sunday. Good bye, dear lady, and believe me yours in the most friendly manner.

W. M. T.

[*Reply to an invitation to dinner, a few days later.*]

Had I but ten minutes sooner
  Got your hospitable line,
'Twould have been delight and honour
  With a gent like you to dine;—
But my word is passed to others,
  Fitz, he is engagëd too:
Agony my bosom smothers,
  As I write adieu, adieu!

[*Lines sent in a note of about this date.*]

I was making this doggerel instead of writing my *Punch* this morning, shall I send *it or no?*

'Tis one o'clock, the boy from *Punch* is sitting in the passage here,
It used to be the hour of lunch at Portman Street, near Portman Squeer.

O! stupid little printers' boy, I cannot write, my head is queer,
And all my foolish brains employ in thinking of a lady dear.
It was but yesterday, and on my honest word it seems a year—
As yet that person was not gone, as yet I saw that lady dear—
She's left us now, my boy, and all this town, this life, is blank and drear.
Thou printers' devil in the hall, didst ever see my lady dear,
You'd understand, you little knave, I think, if you could only see her,
Why now I look so glum and grave for losing of this lady dear.
A lonely man I am in life, my business is to joke and jeer,
A lonely man without a wife, God took from me a lady dear.
A friend I had, and at his side,—the story dates from seven long year—
One day I found a blushing bride, a tender lady kind and dear!
They took me in, they pitied me, they gave me kindly words and cheer,
A kinder welcome who shall see, than yours, O, friend and lady dear?

The rest is wanting.

1848.

[*To Mr. Brookfield.*]

MY DEAR VIEUX:

When I came home last night I found a beautiful opera ticket for this evening,—Jenny Lind, charming *bally*, box 72.—I am going to dine at home with the children and shall go to the opera, and will leave your name down below. Do come and we will sit, we 2, and see the piece like 2 lords, and we can do the other part afterwards. I present my respectful compliments to Mrs. Brookfield and am yours,

W. M. T.

If you can come to dinner, there's a curry.

Oct. 4th 1848

DEAR MRS. BROOKFIELD:

If you would write me a line to say that you made a good journey and were pretty well, to Sir Thomas Cullam's, Hardwick, Bury St. Edmunds, you would confer indeed a favour on yours respectfully. William dined here last night and was pretty cheerful. As I passed by Portman Street, after you were gone, just to take a look up at the windows, the usual boy started forward to take the horse. I laughed a sad laugh. I didn't want nobody to take the horse. It's a long time since you were away. The cab is at the door to take me to the railroad. Mrs. Procter was very kind and Adelaide sympathised with me. I have just opened my desk, there are all the papers I had at Spa—*Pendennis*, unread since, and your letter. Good bye dear Mrs. Brookfield, always yours,

W. M. T.

L'homme propose. Since this was wrote the author went to the railroad, found that he arrived a minute too late, and that there were no trains for 4½ hours. So I came back into town and saw the publishers, who begged and implored me so, not to go out pleasuring, &c., that I am going to Brighton instead of Bury. I looked in the map, I was thinking of coming to Weston - Super - Mare,—only it seemed such a hint.

[Club]

[*To Mr. Brookfield*]

October 1848.

MY DEAR REVERENCE:

I take up the pen to congratulate you on the lovely weather, which must, with the company of those to whom you are attached, render your stay at Clevedon* so delightful. It snowed here this morning, since which there has been a fog succeeded by a drizzly rain. I have passed the day writing and trying to alter Pendennis, which is without any manner of doubt, awfully stupid; the very best passages, which pleased the author only last week, looking hideously dull by the dull fog of this day. I pray, I pray, that it may be the weather. Will you say something for it at church next Sunday?

My old parents arrived last night, it was quite a sight to see the poor old mother with the children: and Bradbury, the printer, coming to dun me for Pendennis this morning. I slunk away from home, where writing is an utter impossi-

---

* Clevedon Court, Somersetshire, often referred to in these letters, and already mentioned in the note p. 7, the home of Sir Charles Elton, Mrs. Brookfield's father.

Clevedon Court dates from the reign of Edward II. (1307 to 1327), and though added to and altered in Elizabeth's time, the original plan can be clearly traced and much of the 14th Century work is untouched. The manor of Clevedon passed into the hands of the Eltons in 1709, the present possessor being Sir Edmund Elton, 8th Baronet.

The manor-house is the original of Castlewood in *Esmond*.

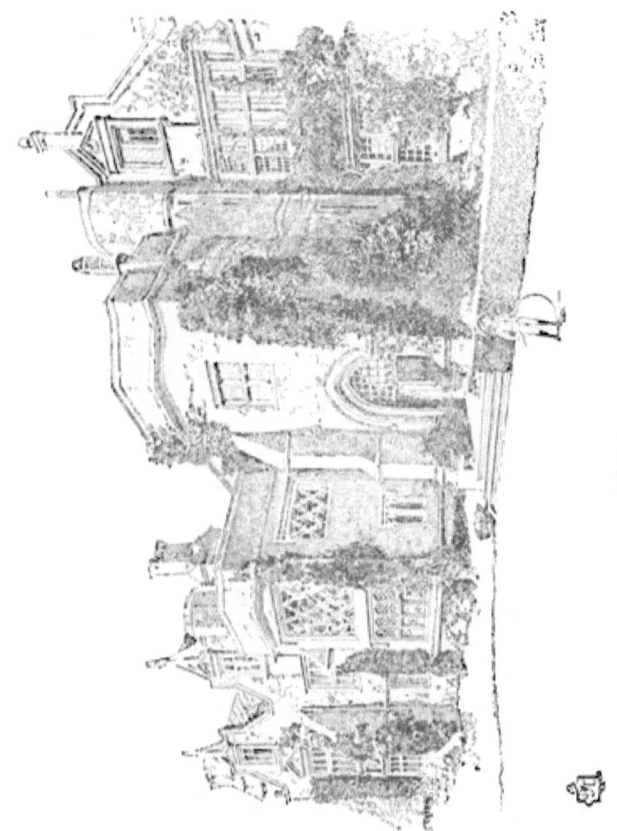
CLEVEDON COURT.

bility, and have been operating on it here. The real truth is now, that there is half an hour before dinner, and I don't know what to do, unless I write you a screed, to pass away the time. There are secret and selfish motives in the most seemingly generous actions of men.

T'other day I went to Harley Street and saw the most beautiful pair of embroidered slippers, worked for a lady at whose feet . ; and I begin more and more to think

holding any more, with dog & gun? to come & see him — up field sports ... Do you remark all that elaborate shading the shot &c. ? — all that has been done to while away the time until the dinner's ready : and when say bo**r** Harry Hallam go and I should like shoot, and in fact get through him and others

Adelaide Procter, an uncommonly nice, dear, good girl. Old Dilke of the *Athenæum*, vows that Procter and his wife, between them, wrote *Jane Eyre*, and when I protest ignorance, says, "Pooh! you know who wrote it, you are the deepest rogue in England, &c." I wonder whether it can be true? It is just possible, and then what a singular circumstance is the ✚ fire of the two dedications.* *O! Mon Dieu!* but I wish *Pendennis* were better.

As if I had not enough to do, I have begun to blaze away in the *Chronicle* again : its an awful bribe—that five guineas

---

* *Jane Eyre* to Thackeray, *Vanity Fair* to Barry Cornwall.

an article. After I saw you on Sunday I did actually come back straight, on the omnibus. I have been to the Cider Cellars since again to hear the man sing about going to be hanged, I have had a headache afterwards, I have drawn, I have written, I have distracted my mind with healthy labor. Now wasn't this much better than plodding about with you in heavy boots amidst fields and woods? But unless you come back, and as soon as my work is done, I thought a day or two would be pleasantly spent in your society, if the house of Clevedon admits of holding any more.

Does Harry Hallam go out with dog and gun? I should like to come and see him shoot, and in fact, get up field sports through him and others. Do you remark all that elaborate shading, the shot &c.,? All that has been done to while away the time until the dinner's ready, and upon my conscience I believe it is very near come. Yes, it is 6½. If Mrs. Parr is at Clevedon, present the respects of Mephistopheles, as also to any other persons with whom I am acquainted in your numerous and agreeable family circle.

1848

[*To Mr. Brookfield.*]

Va diner chez ton classique ami, tant renommé pour le Grec. Je ne pourrais mieux faire que de passer la soirée avec une famille que j'ai negligée quelque peu—la mienne. Oui, Monsieur, dans les caresses innocentes de mes enfans chèris, dans la conversation édifiante de Monsieur mon beau-père, je tacherai de me consoler de ta seconde infidelité. Samedi je ne puis venir : J'ai d'autres engagemens auxquels je ne veux pas manquer. Va. Sois heureux. Je te pardonne.

Ton mélancholique ami
CHEVALIER DE TITMARSH.

[*1st November*, 1848.]

DEAR MRS. BROOKFIELD:

I was at Oxford by the time your dinner was over, and found eight or nine jovial gentlemen in black, feasting in the common room and drinking port wine solemnly. . . . We had a great sitting of Port wine, and I daresay the evening was pleasant enough. They gave me a bed in College, —such a bed, I could not sleep. Yesterday, (for this is half past seven o'clock in the morning, would you believe it?) a party of us drove in an Oxford Cart to Blenheim, where we saw some noble pictures, a portrait by Raphael, one of the great Raphaels of the world,—(Look, this is college paper, with beautiful lines already made)—A series of magnificent Rubens, one of which, representing himself walking in a garden with Mrs. Rubens and the baby, did one good to look at and remember; and some very questionable Titians indeed—I mean on the score of authenticity, not of morals, though the subjects are taken from the loves of those extraordinary gods and goddesses, mentioned in Lemprière's Dictionary,—and we walked in the park, with much profit; surveying the great copper-coloured trees, and the glum old bridge and pillar and Rosamond's Well; and the queer, grand, ugly but magnificent house, a piece of splendid barbarism, yet grand and imposing somehow, like a chief raddled over with war-paint, and attired with careful hideousness. Well, I can't make out the simile on paper, though it's in my own mind pretty clear. What you would have liked best was the chapel dedicated to God and the Duke of Marlborough. The monument to the latter, occupies the whole place, almost, so that the former is quite secondary. O! what comes? It was the scout who brought me your letter, and I am very much obliged to you for it. . . .

I was very sorry indeed to hear that you have been ill—I was afraid the journey would agitate you, that was what I was thinking of as I was lying in the Oxford man's bed awake.

After Blenheim I went to Magdalen Chapel to a High Mass there. O cherubim and seraphim, how you would like it! The chapel is the most sumptuous edifice, carved and frittered all over with the richest stone-work like the lace of a lady's boudoir. The windows are fitted with pictures of the saints painted in a grey colour,—real Catholic saints, male and female I mean, so that I wondered how they got there; and this makes a sort of rich twilight in the church, which is lighted up by a multitude of wax candles in gold sconces, and you say your prayers in carved stalls wadded with velvet cushions. They have a full chorus of boys, some two dozen I should think, who sing quite ravishingly. It is a sort of perfection of sensuous gratification; children's voices charm me so, that they set all my sensibilities into a quiver; do they you? I am sure they do. These pretty brats with sweet innocent voices and white robes, sing quite celestially; —no, not celestially, for I don't believe it is devotion at all, but a high delight out of which one comes, not impurified I hope, but with a thankful pleased gentle frame of mind! I suppose I have a great faculty of enjoyment. At Clevedon I had gratification in looking at trees, landscapes, effects of shine and shadow &c., which made that dear old Inspector who walked with me, wonder. Well there can be no harm in this I am sure. What a shame it is to go on bragging about what is after all sheer roaring good health for the most part; and now I am going to breakfast. Good bye. I have been lionising the town ever since, and am come home quite tired. I have breakfasted here, lunched at Christ Church, seen Merton, and All Souls with Norman Macdonald, where there is a beautiful library and a boar's head in the kitchen, over which it was good to see Norman's eyes gloating; and it being All Saints' day, I am going to chapel here, where they have also a very good music I am told.

Are you better ma'am? I hope you are. On Friday I hope to have the pleasure to see you, and am till then, and even till Saturday,

Yours,

W. M. T.

[29th Nov: 1848.]

MY DEAR LADY:

I am very much pained and shocked at the news brought at dinner to-day that poor dear Charles Buller is gone. Good God! think about the poor mother surviving, and what an anguish that must be! If I were to die I cannot bear to think of my mother living beyond me, as I daresay she will. But isn't it an awful, awful, sudden summons? There go wit, fame, friendship, ambition, high repute! Ah! *aimons nous bien.* It seems to me that is the only thing we can carry away. When we go, let us have some who love us wherever we are. I send you this little line as I tell you and William most things. Good night.

Tuesday. [Nov. 1848.]

GOOD NIGHT MY DEAR MADAM.

Since I came home from dining with Mr. Morier, I have been writing a letter to Mr. T. Carlyle and thinking about other things as well as the letter all the time; and I have read over a letter I received to-day which apologizes for everything and whereof the tremulous author ceaselessly doubts and misgives. Who knows whether she is not converted by Joseph Bullar by this time. She is a sister of mine, and her name is God bless her.

Wednesday. I was at work until seven o'clock; not to very much purpose, but executing with great labour and hardship the days work. Then I went to dine with Dr. Hall, the crack doctor here, a literate man, a traveller, and otherwise a kind bigwig. After dinner we went to hear Mr. Sortain lecture, of whom you may perhaps have heard me speak, as a great, remarkable orator and preacher of the Lady Huntingdon Connexion. (The paper is so greasy that I am forced to try several pens and manners of handwriting, but none will do.) We had a fine lecture with brilliant Irish metaphors and outbursts of rhetoric addressed to an assembly of mechanics, shopboys and young women, who could not, and perhaps had best not, understand that flashy speaker. It was about the origin of nations he spoke, one of those big themes on which a man may talk eternally and with a never ending outpouring of words; and he talked magnificently, about the Arabs for the most part, and tried to prove that because the Arabs acknowledged their descent from Ishmael or Esau, therefore the Old Testament History was true. But the Arabs may have had Esau for a father and yet the bears may not have eaten up the little children for quizzing Elisha's bald head. As I was writing to Carlyle last night, (I haven't sent the letter as usual, and shall not most likely,) Saint Stephen was pelted to death by Old Testaments, and Our Lord was killed like a felon by the law, which He came to repeal. I was thinking about Joseph Bullar's doctrine after I went to bed, founded on what I cannot but think a blasphemous asceticism, which has obtained in the world ever so long, and which is disposed to curse, hate and undervalue the world altogether. Why should we? What we see here of this world is but an expression of God's will, so to speak—a beautiful earth and sky and sea—beautiful affections and sorrows, wonderful changes and developments of creation, suns rising, stars shining, birds singing, clouds and shadows changing and fading, people loving each other, smiling and crying, the multiplied phenomena of Nature, multiplied in fact and fancy, in Art and Science, in every way that a man's intellect or education or imagination can be brought to bear.—And who is to say that we are to ignore all this, or not value them and love them, because there is another unknown world yet to come? Why that unknown future world is but a manifestation of God Almighty's will, and a development of Nature, neither more nor less than this in which we are, and an angel glorified or a sparrow on a gutter are equally parts of His creation. The light upon all the saints in Heaven is just as much and no more God's work, as the sun which shall shine to-morrow upon this infinitesimal speck of creation, and under which I shall read, please God, a letter from my kindest Lady and friend. About my future state I don't know; I leave it in the disposal of the awful Father,—but for to-day I thank God that I can love you, and that you yonder and others besides are thinking of me with a tender regard. Hallelujah may be greater in degree than this, but not in kind, and countless ages of stars may be blazing infinitely, but you and I have a right to rejoice and believe in our little part and to trust in to-day as in tomorrow. God bless my dear lady and her husband. I hope you are asleep now, and I must go too, for the candles are just winking out.

Thursday. I am glad to see among the new inspectors, in the Gazette in this morning's papers, my old acquaintance Longueville Jones, an excellent, worthy, lively, accomplished fellow, whom I like the better because he flung up his fellow and tutorship at Cambridge in order to marry on nothing a year. We worked in Galignani's newspaper for ten francs a day, very cheerfully ten years ago, since when he has been a schoolmaster, taken pupils or bid for them, and battled manfully with fortune. William will be sure to like him, I think, he is so honest, and cheerful. I have sent off my letter to Lady Ashburton this morning, ending with some pretty phrases about poor old C. B. whose fate affects me very much, so much that I feel as if I were making my will and getting ready to march too. Well ma'am, I have as good a right to presentiments as you have, and to sickly fancies and despondencies; but I should like to see before I die, and think of it daily more and more, the commencement of Jesus Christ's christianism in the world, where I am sure people may be made a hundred times happier than by its present forms, Judaism, asceticism, Bullarism. I wonder will He come again and tell it us. We are taught to be ashamed of our best feelings all our life. I don't want to blubber upon everybody's shoulders; but to have a good will for all, and a strong, very strong regard for a few, which I shall not be ashamed to own to them. . . . It is near upon three o'clock, and I am getting rather anxious about the post from Southampton *via* London. Why, if it doesn't come in, you won't get any letter to-morrow, no, nothing—and I made so sure. Well, I will try and go to work, it is only one more little drop. God bless you, dear lady. . . .

. . . *Friday.* I have had a good morning's work and at two o'clock comes your letter; dear friend, thank you. What a coward I was, I will go and walk and be happy for an hour, it is a grand frosty sunshine. Tomorrow morning early back to London.

31 January, 1849
SHIP, DOVER.

Just before going away.

How long is it since I have written to you in my natural handwriting? . . . I am so far on my way to Paris, Meurice's Hotel, Rue de Rivoli. . . . I had made up my mind to this great, I may say decisive step, when I came to see you on Saturday, before you went to Hither Green. I didn't go to the Sterling, as it was my last day, and due naturally to the family. We went to bed at half past nine o'clock. To-day I went round on a circuit of visits, including Turpin at your house. It seems as if I was going on an ever so long journey. Have you any presentiments? I know some people who have. Thank you for your note of this morning, and my dear old William for his regard for me; try you and conserve the same. . . . There is a beautiful night, and I am going by Calais. Here, with a step on the steaming vessel,

I am, affectionately yours,

W. M. T.

Meurice's Hotel, Rivoli Street,
Paris. [*Feb:* 1849.]

If you please, I am come home very tired and sleepy from the Opera, where my friend Rothschild gave me a place in his box. There was a grand *ballet* of which I could not understand one word, that is one *pas*, for not a word was spoken; and I saw some celebrities in the place. The President, M. Lamartine, in a box near a handsome lady; M. Marrast, in a box near a handsome lady; there was one with a bouquet of lilies, or some sort of white flowers, so enormous that it looked like a bouquet in a pantomine, which was to turn into something, or out of which a beautiful dancer was to spring. The house was crammed with well-dressed folks, and is sumptuous and splendid beyond measure. But O! think of old Lamartine in a box by a handsome lady. Not any harm in the least, that I know of, only that the most venerable and grizzled bearded statesmen and philosophers find time from their business and political quandaries, to come and sigh and ogle a little at the side of ladies in boxes.

I am undergoing the quarantine of family dinners with the most angelic patience. Yesterday being the first day, it was an old friend and leg of lamb. I graciously said to the old friend, "Why the deuce wouldn't you let me go and dine at a restaurant, don't you suppose I have leg of lamb at home?" To-day with an aunt of mine, where we had mock turtle soup, by Heavens! and I arranged with my other aunt for another dinner. I knew how it would be; it must be; and there's my cousin to come off yet, who says, "you must come and dine. I haven't a soul, but will give you a good Indian dinner." I will make a paper in *Punch* about it, and exhale my griefs in print. I will tell you about my cousin when I get home,—when I get to Portman Street that is. . . . What brought me to this place? Well I am glad I came, it will give me a subject for at least six weeks in *Punch*, of which I was getting so weary that I thought I must have done with it.

Are you better for a little country air? Did you walk in that cheerful paddock where the cows are? And did you have clothes enough to your bed? I shall go to mine now, after writing this witty page, for I have been writing and spinning about all day, and am very tired and sleepy if you please. *Bon Soir, Madame.* . . .

Saturday. Though there is no use in writing, because there is no post, but *que voulez vous, Madame? On aime à dire un petit bonjour à ses amis.* I feel almost used to the place already and begin to be interested about the politics. Some say there's a revolution ready for today. The town is crammed with soldiers, and one has a curious feeling of interest and excitement, as in walking about on ice that is rather dangerous, and may tumble in at any moment. I had three newspapers for my breakfast, which my man,) it is rather grand having a *laquais de place*, but I can't do without him, and invent all sorts of pretexts to employ him) bought for five pence of your money. The mild papers say we have escaped an immense danger, a formidable plot has been crushed, and Paris would have been on fire and fury but for the timely discovery. The Red Republicans say, "Plot! no such thing, the infernal tyrants at the head of affairs wish to find a pretext for persecuting patriots, and the good and the brave are shut up in dungeons." Plot or no plot, which is it? I think I prefer to believe that there has been a direful conspiracy, and that we have escaped a tremendous danger. It makes one feel brave somehow, and as if one had some merit in overthrowing this rascally conspiracy. I am going to the Chamber directly. The secretary at the Embassy got me a ticket. The Embassy is wonderfully civil; Lord Normanby is my dearest friend, he is going to take me to the President, —very likely to ask me to dinner. You would have thought

I was an earl, I was received with so much of *empressement* by the ambassador.

I hadn't been in Paris ten minutes, before I met ten people of my acquaintance. . . . As for —— Oh! it was wonderful. We have not met for five years on account of a coolness,—that is a great heat,—resulting out of a dispute in which I was called to be umpire and gave judgment against her and her husband; but we have met, it is forgotten. . . . Poor soul, she performed beautifully. "What, William, not the least changed, just the same as ever, in spite of all your fame?"—Fame be hanged, thought I, *pardonnez-moi le mot*,—"just the same simple creature." O! what a hypocrite I felt. I like her too; but she poor, poor soul—well, she did her comedy exceedingly well. I could only say, "My dear, you have grown older," that was the only bit of truth that passed, and she didn't like it. *Quand vous serez bien vieille*, and I say to you, "my dear you are grown old" (only I shall not say "my dear," but something much more distant and respectful), I wonder whether you will like it. Now it is time to go to the Chamber, but it was far pleasanter to sit and chatter with Madame.

I have been to see a piece of a piece called the *Mystères de Londres*, since the above, and most tremendous mysteries they were indeed. It appears that there lived in London, three or four years ago, a young grandee of Spain and count of the Empire, the Marquis of Rio Santo, an Irishman by birth, who in order to free his native country from the intolerable tyranny of England, imagined to organize an extraordinary conspiracy of the rogues and thieves of the metropolis, with whom some of the principal merchants, jewellers and physicians were concerned, who were to undermine and destroy somehow the infamous British power. The merchants were to forge and utter bank-notes, the jewellers to sell sham diamonds to the aristocracy, and so ruin them; the physi-

[From a drawing by Thackeray in the possession of Mrs. Brookfield.]

cians to murder suitable persons by their artful prescriptions, and the whole realm being plunged into anarchy by their manœuvres, Ireland was to get its own in the midst of the squabble. This astonishing marquis being elected supreme chief of a secret society called the "Gentlemen of the Night," had his spies and retainers among the very highest classes of society. The police and the magistrature were corrupted, the very beef-eaters of the Queen contaminated, and you saw the evidence of such a conspiracy as would make your eyes open with terror. Who knows, madame, but perhaps some of the school inspectors themselves were bought over, and a Jesuitic C——k, an ambitious T——, an unscrupulous B—— himself, may have been seduced to mislead our youth, and teach our very babes and sucklings a precocious perverseness? This is getting to be so very like print that I shall copy it very likely,* all but the inspector part, for a periodical with which I am connected. Well, numbers of beautiful women were in love with the Marquis, or otherwise subjugated by him, and the most lovely and innocent of all, was employed to go to St. James' on a drawing-room day, and steal the diamonds of Lady Brompton, the mistress of his grace Prince Demetri Tolstoi, the Russian ambassador, who had lent Lady Brompton the diamonds to sport at St. James', before he sent them off to his imperial master the Emperor of Russia, for whom the trifles in question were purchased. Lady Brompton came to court having her train held up by her jockey; Susanna came to court, her train likewise carried by her page, one or both of them were *affidés* of the association of the "Gentlemen of the Night." The jockeys were changed, and Lady Brompton's jewels absolutely taken off her neck. So great was the rage of his grace Prince Demetri Tolstoi, that he threatened war should be declared by his emperor unless the brilliants were restored. I don't know what supervened,

* He *did* reproduce part of it in *Punch*.

for exhausted nature would bear no more. But you should
have seen the Court of St. James', the beef-eaters, the Life
Guards, the heralds at arms in their tabards of the sixteenth
century, and the ushers announcing the great folks, as they
went into the presence of the great sovereign. Lady Campbell, the Countess of Derby, and the Archbishop of Canterbury were announced. O! such an archbishop! he had on
a velvet trencher cap, and a dress something like our real
and venerated prelates', and a rich curling wig, and he
stopped and blessed the people, making crucificial signs
on the stairs. The various lords went into the chamber
in red robes and long flowing wigs. The wonder of the
parody was, that it was so like and yet so absurdly unlike. O'Connell appeared, saluted as Daniel by the Count
of Rio Santo, and announcing that he himself, though *brisé
par la lutte* with the oppressors of his country, yet strongly
reprobated anything like violent measures on the part of M.
de Rio Santo and his fellow-patriots. The band played
" God safe the Quin " in the most delightful absurd manner.
The best of it is that these things, admirably as they tickled
me, are only one degree more absurd than what they pretend
to copy. The Archbishop had a wig only the other day,
though not quite such a wig as this; the chiefs of the police
came in with oilskin hats, policemen's coats quite correct, and
white tights and silk stockings, which made me laugh so, that
the people in the stalls next me didn't know what I was at!
But the parody was in fine prodigious, and will afford matter
to no end of penny-a-line speculation. . . . I sit in my
little snug room and say God bless you and Mr. Williams.
Here is near four pages of Pendennis. . .

April, 10th. 1849.

MY DEAR PERSONS.—After lying in bed until you had reached Clifton, exceeding melancholy from want of sleep, (induced by no romantic inward feeling but by other causes much more material and vulgar, viz., late smoking, etc., previous nights) shall I tell you what it was dissipated my blue devils? As I was going toward London the postman stopped me in the street and asked me if I would take my letters, which he handed to me:—one was an opera-box which I sent off to Mrs. M. for to morrow; and one was a letter from an attorney demanding instantly £112 for that abominable Irish Railway; and in presence of this real calamity all the sentimental ones vanished straight. I began to think how I must raise the money,—how I must go to work, nor be shilly-shallying any longer; and with this real care staring me in the face I began to forget imaginary grievances and to think about going to work immediately; and how for the next 3 months I must screw and save in order to pay off the money. And this is the way, M'am, that the grim duties of the world push the soft feelings aside; we've no time to be listening to *their* little meek petitions and tender home prattle in presence of the imperative Duty who says " Come, come, no more of this here,—get to work, Mister "—and so we go and join the working gang, behind which Necessity marches cracking his whip. This metaphor has not been worked so completely as it might be, but it means that I am resolved to go to work directly. So being determined on this I went off at once to the Star and Garter at Richmond and dined with those 2 nice women and their husbands, viz, the Strutts and Romillys. We had every sort of luxury for dinner, and afterwards talked about Vanity Fair and Pendennis almost incessantly (though I declare I led away the conversation at least 10 times, but they would come back) so that the evening was uncommonly pleasant. Once, twice, thrice, it came into my head—I wonder what those people at Clifton are doing; I would give 2/6 to be with them; but in the mean while it must be confessed, the Star and Garter is not bad. These ladies are handsome and good, and clever, and kind; that solicitor general talks with great pleasantness; and so I came home in a fly with an old gentleman who knew Sir S. Romilly, and we talked of the dark end of that history of a very good and wise man, and how he adored his wife (it was her death which caused his suicide), and how his son was equally attached to his own, of whose affection for her husband my informer gave many pretty instances. This conversation brought me to Kensington, where after thinking about the £112 a little, and a little more about some friends of mine whom I pray God to make happy, I fell into a great big sleep—from which I wake at this present 8 o'clock in the morning to say Bon jour, Madame. Where do you think this is wrote from? From an attorney's office, Old Jewry. The Lord Mayor, the Sheriffs, their coaches and footmen, in gold and silk stockings, have just passed in a splendid procession through the mud and pouring rain. I have been to the bankers to see how much money I have got. I have got £120; I owe £112; from £120 take £112, leaves 8 for the rest of the month. Isn't that pleasant? Well, but I know how to raise some;—the bankers say I may over-draw. Things isn't so bad.

But now, (this is from the Garrick Club) now I say for the wonderful wonder of wonders. There is a chance for Mr. Williams such as he little looked for. EMMA is free. The great Catastrophe has happened—last night she and her mother fled from the infamous R. and took refuge at Mrs. Procter's where they had Adelaide's and Agnes' beds—who went and slept with Mr. and Mrs. Goldsmid next door. Mr. and Mrs. P. called at Kensington at 11 o'clock and brought the news.* R. had treated his wife infamously; R. had assailed her with the most brutal language and outrages;—that innocent woman Madame G——, poor thing, who meddled with nothing and remained all day in her own garret so as to give no trouble, was flung out of the house by him—indeed only stayed in order to protect her daughter's life. The brute refused to allow the famous picture to be exhibited—in fact is a mad-man and a ruffian. Procter and I went off to make peace, and having heard R.'s story, I believe that he has been more wronged than they.

The mother in-law is at the bottom of the mischief. It was she who made the girl marry R., and, the marriage made, she declined leaving her daughter; in fact, the poor devil, who has a bad temper, a foolish head—an immense vanity—has been victimised by the women and I pity him a great deal more than them. O! what a comedy it would make! but the separation I suppose is final, and it will be best for both parties. It will end no doubt in his having to pay a 4th of his income for the pleasure of being a month married to her, and she will be an angelic martyr, &c. I wonder whether you will give me a luncheon on Thursday. I might stop for 2 hours on my way to Taunton and make you my hand-shake. This would be very nice. I thought of writing to Mrs. Elton and offering myself, but I should like first to have the approval of Mr. Williams, for after all, I am not an indifferent person but claim to rank as the Afft. brother of both of you.

W. M. T.

* Mrs. Procter, the wife of the well-known poet, Barry Cornwall,—herself a most accomplished woman.—Even now at 84 years of age she retains the brilliant powers of conversation for which she was always celebrated. She was always a faithful friend to Mr. Thackeray, who had a sincere regard for her. Mrs. Procter was the mother of Adelaide, who so largely inherited her father's poetic powers.

Fragment.

[*April*, 1849.]

Yesterday's wasn't a letter, you know, ma'am; and I am so tired now of penmanship, that I don't think I shall be able to get through one. I wish you were on the sofa in Portman Street, and that I could go and lie down on the opposite one and fall asleep. Isn't that a polite wish? Well, I am so beat that I ought to go to bed, and not inflict my yawns upon anyone; but I can't begin snoring yet. I am waiting at the Club, till the printer's boy brings the proofs of No. 7,* which is all done; there are two new women in it, not like anybody that you know or I know; your favourite Major appears rather in an amiable light, I don't know whether it is good or bad. The latter probably. Well, it is done, that's a comfort. . . .

I am going to dine with Lady Davy again, but Friday shall be a happy Friday for me, and on Saturday, when you go to Oxbridge, I shall console myself by a grand dinner at the Royal Academy, if you please, to which they have invited me, on a great card like a tea-tray. That's a great honour, none but bishops, purchasers, and other big-wigs are asked. I daresay I shall have to make an impromptu speech. Shall I come to rehearse it to you on Friday? I was going to send you a letter t'other day from a sculptor who wants to make my bust; think of that! . . .

Here is wonderful Spring weather come, and the leaves are sprouting and all the birds chirping melojoyously.

I daresay you are driving by Severn's Shore, now; then you will listen after dinner to Captain Budd on the German flute; then I daresay you will sing, after a great deal of blushing and hesitation. Is Mrs. Tidy jealous of you? I dare-

* Pendennis.

say she thinks you are overrated, and wonders what people see in you. So do I. . . .

Tomorrow me and Annie and Minnie are going to buy a new *gownd* for Granny, who wants it very much. Those old folks project a tour to Switzerland in the Summer, did I tell you? And my mother cannot part with the children, who must go too. Where shall I go? . . .

Here comes the proof;—shall I send this letter now or wait till tomorrow, and have something to say? perhaps I shall see William tonight. I am going to Lady Lovelace's drum in Cumberland Place, hard-by Portman Street.

No, I didn't go, but came home and fell asleep after dinner, from nine o'clock till now, which it is eight o'clock in the morning, which I am writing in bed. You are very likely looking at the elms out of window by this time; are they green yet? Our medlar tree is. I was to have gone to the old Miss Berrys' too last night; they were delighted at the allusion in *Punch* to them, in the same number in which you appear mending waistcoats. But Lord what a much better thing going to bed was! and No. 7 completed with great throes and disquiet, only yesterday—seems to me ever so long ago—such a big sleep have I had! . . .

Adelaide Procter would hardly shake hands with me because of my cowardly conduct in the R—— affair, and she told me that I hadn't been to call there since the 28th March last. They keep a journal of visitors; fancy that! I heard the R—— story from the G—— herself and the mother, and can only make out now that the husband is mad and odious. What they are to do is the difficulty; he refuses to allow her a shilling; her picture has been rejected at the Academy, and why I can't see, for there's no English academician's who could equal it, and she must paint to live. I shall give her my mother to do, I think. She looked exceedingly handsome and interesting the other day; pale and grief-stricken, with her enormous hair twirled round her head—and yet, and yet! Will you kiss those little maids for me, I should like to hear their prattle through the door. I am going to kill Mrs. Pendennis presently, and have her ill in this number. Minnie says, "O! papa, do make her well again; she can have a regular doctor and be almost dead, and then will come a homeopathic physician who will make her well you know." It is very pretty to see her with her grandmother. Let us jump up now and go to breakfast with the children.

June 12, 1849.

My dear Lady:

I send a hasty line to say that the good old aunt is still here, and was very glad to see me and another nephew of hers who came by the same train. It's a great comfort to my mother and to her, that my mother should be with her at this last day; and she is preparing to go out of the world, in which she has been living very virtuously for more than eighty years, as calmly and happily as may be. I don't know how long she may remain, but my duty will be to stay on I suppose, until the end, which the doctor says is very near; though to see her in her bed, cheerful and talking, one would fancy that her summons is not so near as those who are about her imagine. So I shall not see London or my dear friends in it for a few days very likely. Meanwhile will you write me a line here to tell me that you are easier of your pains, and just to give a comfort to your old brother Makepeace.

I suppose I shall do a great deal of my month's work here. I have got a comfortable room at a little snug country inn, such as William would like. I am always thinking about going to see Mrs. Fanshawe at Southampton, about No. 9 of

Pendennis, and about all sorts of things. I went to see Mrs. Procter, to the City, and to do my business and pay my horrid railroad money. The banker's clerk stopped me and said, "I beg your pardon, Sir, but will you, if you please, tell me the meaning of 'œsthetics,'" which I was very much puzzled to tell—and here comes the boy to say that the note must go this instant to save the post, and so God bless Jane my sister and William my brother.

Written from the Royal oak, Fareham.

From the old shop, 21.

[1849]

Is it pouring with rain at Park Lodge, and the most dismal, wretched, cat and dog day ever seen? O! it's gloomy at 13 Young Street! I have been labouring all day—drawing that is, and doing my plates, till my &s are ready to drop off for weariness. But they must not stop for yet a little while, and until I have said how do you do to my dear lady and the young folks at Southampton. I hardly had time to know I was gone, and that happy fortnight was over, till this morning. At the train, whom do you think I found? Miss G—— who says she is Blanche Amory, and I think she is Blanche Amory; amiable at times, amusing, clever and depraved. We talked and persiflated all the way to London, and the idea of her will help me to a good chapter, in which I will make Pendennis and Blanche play at being in love, such a wicked false humbugging London love, as two *blasé* London people might act, and half deceive themselves that they were in earnest. That will complete the cycle of Mr. Pen's worldly experiences, and then we will make, or try and make, a good man of him. O! me, we are wicked worldlings most of us, may God better us and cleanse us!

I wonder whether ever again, I shall have such a happy peaceful fortnight as that last! How sunshiny the landscape remains in my mind, I hope for always; and the smiles of dear children. . . . I can hardly see as I write for the eye-water, but it isn't with grief, but for the natural pathos of the thing. How happy your dear regard makes me, how it takes off the solitude and eases it; may it continue, pray God, till your head is white as mine, and our children have children of their own. Instead of being unhappy because that delightful holiday is over or all but over, I intend that the thoughts of it should serve to make me only the more cheerful and help me, please God, to do my duty better. All such pleasures ought to brace and strengthen one against work days, and lo, here they are. I hope you will be immensely punctual at breakfast and dinner, and do all your business of life with cheerfulness and briskness, after the example of holy Philip Neri, whom you wot of; that is your duty Madame, and mine is to "pursue my high calling;" and so I go back to it with a full grateful heart, and say God bless all. If it hadn't been pouring-o'-rain so, I think I should have gone off to His Reverence at Brighton; so I send him my very best regards, and a whole box full of kisses to the children. Farewell.

Note from Thackeray (actual size).

[*To Mr. Brookfield.*]

25 April 1849.

MY DEAR VIEUX:

Will ye dine with me on Friday at the G? My work will be just over on that day, and bedad, we'll make a night of it, and go to the play. On Thursday I shall dine here and Sunday most *probbly*, and shall we go to Richmond on Sunday? Make your game and send me word.

Ever yours,

W. M. T.

P. S. Having occasion to write to a man in Bloomsbury Place, and to Lady Davy, I mixed up the addresses and am too mean to throw away the envelope, so give you the benefit of the same.

[1849.]

Monday.

My letter to-day, dear lady, must needs be a very short one, for the post goes in half an hour, and I've been occupied all day with my own business and other people's. At three o'clock, just as I was in full work comes a letter from a *protegée* of my mother's, a certain Madame de B. informing me that she, Madame de B., had it in view to commit suicide immediately, unless she could be in some measure relieved (or releived, which is it?) from her present difficulties. So I have had to post off to this Madame de B., whom I expected to find starving, and instead met a woman a great deal fatter than the most full-fed person need be, and having just had a good dinner; but that didn't prevent her, the confounded old fiend, from abusing the woman who fed her and was good to her, from spoiling the half of a day's work for me, and taking me of a fool's errand. I was quite angry, instead of a corpse perhaps, to find a fat and voluble person who had no more idea of hanging herself to the bed-post than you or I have. However, I got a character in making Madame de B's acquaintance, and some day she will turn up in that inevitable repertory of all one's thoughts and experiences *que vous savez*.

Thence, as it was near, I went to see a sick poetess, who is pining away for love of S—— M——, that you have heard of, and who literally has been brought near to the grave by that amorous malady. She is very interesting somehow, ghastly pale and thin, recumbent on a sofa, and speaking scarcely above her breath. I wonder though after all, was it the love, or was it the bronchitis, or was it the chest or the spine that was affected? All I know is that Don Saville may have made love to her once, but has tried his hand in other quarters since, and you know one doesn't think the worse of a man of honour for cheating in affairs of the heart. The numbers that I myself have—fiddledee, this is nonsense.

The Reform banquet was very splendid and dull enough. A bad dinner and bad wine, and pretty fair speaking; my friend fat James being among not the least best of the speakers. They all speak in a kind of sing-song or chant, without which I suppose it is impossible for the orator nowadays to pitch his sentences, and Madam, you are aware that the Romans had a pipe when they spoke; not a pipe such as your husband uses, but a pitch-pipe. I wanted to have gone to smoke a last calumet at poor dear old Portman Street, but our speechifiers did not stop till 12.30 and not then; but the best of them had fired off by that time and I came off. Yesterday, after devoting the morning to composition, I went and called on the Rev. W. H. Brookfield, whom I found very busy packing up and wishing me at Jericho, so I went to the Miss Leslies' and Captn. Morgan, the American Captain; and then to dine at Hampstead, where the good natured folks took in me and the two young ones. Finally, in the evening to Lady Tennent's, where I have been most remiss in visit-paying, for I like her, and she was a kind old friend to me. To-day I am going to dine with the Dowager Duchess of Bedford, afterwards to Mrs. Procter's, afterwards to Lady Granville's. Here you have your humble servant's journal, and you see his time is pretty well occupied. I have had a good deal of the children too, and am getting on apace with my number, though I don't like it. Shall I send you some of it? No, I won't, though if I do a very good piece indeed, perhaps I may. I think I shall go to Brighton; I think you will be away six weeks at least; and I hope to hear that my dear lady is well and that she remembers her affectionate old friend

MAKEPEACE.

1849.

[*To Mr. Brookfield*]

MY DEAR VIEUX:

A long walk and stroll in Richmond Park yesterday, a blue followed by a black this morning, have left me calmer, exhausted, but melancholy. I shall dine at the Garrick at seven o'clock or so, and go to the Lyceum afterwards. Come into town if you get this in time and let us go. . . .

Get *David Copperfield*, by Jingo it's beautiful; it beats the yellow chap of this month hollow.

W. M. T.

Will you send me two cigars per bearer? I am working with three pipe-smoking Frenchmen, and I can't smoke their abominations, and I hope Madame is pretty well after her triumphant *début* last night.

[1849]

REFORM CLUB, Tuesday—

MY DEAR LADY:

I write only a word and in the greatest hurry to say I am very well in health. I've been at work, and have written somewhat and done my two plates, which only took two hours; and now that they're done, I feel that I want so to come back to Ryde, I must get a rope or a chain to bind myself down to my desk here.* All the world is out of town— Mrs. Procter not at home, perhaps to my visit,—dear kind

---

* Mr. Thackeray had been spending a few days at Ryde with my brother and his wife, where I was staying.

SKETCH OF MRS. BROOKFIELD.

[From a collection of Thackeray's drawings privately printed for Sir Arthur Elton.]

Kate Perry whom indeed I like with all my heart just packing up to go to Brighton. My Chesterfield loves flown away to Tunbridge Wells, and so I am alone and miss you. I sent your package off to Harry this morning. The lucky rogue! I suppose he will see Madam and all those kind Ryde folks. Tell them if you please how very grateful I am to them for their goodnature. I can't help fancying them relations rather than friends.

I got some dinner; at 10½ o'clock I drank to the health of Madame Ma bonne soeur;—I hadn't the courage to go home till past midnight, when all the servants got out of bed to let me in. There was such a heap of letters! I send you a couple which may amuse you. Send me Colonel Ferguson's back, as I must answer him; but I don't think I shall be able to get away in August to Scotland. Who can the excoriated female be who imparts her anguish to me? what raw wound has the whip of the satirist been touching? As I was sitting with my Frenchmen at 3 o'clock, I thought to myself O Lor! Mr. Makepeace, how much better you were off yesterday!

Good bye dear lady, God bless every kind person of all those who love you.—I feel here, you must know, just as I used five and twenty years ago at school, the day after coming back from the holidays. If you have nothing to say to me, pray write; if you have something, of course you will. Good bye, shake hands, I am always my dear lady's sincere

W. M. T.

[1849]

Last night was a dinner at Spencer Cowper's, the man who used to be called the fortunate youth some few years back, when £10,000, or perhaps £20,000 a year, was suddenly left him by a distant relative, and when he was without a guinea in the world. It was a Sybaritic repast, in a magnificent apartment, and we were all of us young voluptuaries of fashion. There were portraits of Louis Quatorze ladies round the room (I was going to say *salle à manger*, but room after all is as good a word). We sat in the comfortablest arm chairs, and valets went round every instant filling our glasses with the most exquisite liquors. The glasses were as big as at Kinglake's dinner—do you remember Kinglake's feast, Ma'am? Then we adjourned into wadded drawing rooms, all over sofas and lighted with a hundred candles, where smoking was practised, and we enjoyed a pleasant and lively conversation, carried on in the 2 languages of which we young dogs are perfect masters. As I came away at midnight I saw C.'s carriage lamps blazing in the courtyard, keeping watch until the fortunate youth should come out to pay a visit to some Becky no doubt. The young men were clever, very frank and gentlemenlike; one, rather well-read; quite as pleasant companions as one deserves to meet, and as for your humble servant, he saw a chapter or two of Pendennis in some of them.

I am going with M. to-day, to see Alexis the sonnambulist. She came yesterday evening and talked to me for two hours before dinner. I astonished her by finding out her secrets by some of those hits *que vous savez*—Look, here is a bit of paper with a note to her actually commenced in reply to my dearest William,—but I couldn't get out my dearest M. in return, and stopped at " My "—. But I like her better than I did,—and begin to make allowances for a woman of great talents married to a stupid, generous, obstinate, devoted heavy dragoon, thirty years her senior. My dear old mother with her imperial manner tried to take the command of both of them, and was always anxious to make them understand that I was the divinest creature in the world, whose shoe-strings neither of them was fit to tie. Hence bickerings, hatreds, secret jealousies and open revolt, and I can fancy them both worked up to a pitch of hatred of me, that my success in life must have rendered only more bitter.

But about Alexis—this wonder of wonders reads letters and tells you their contents and the names of their authors without even thinking of opening the seal; and I want you very much, if you please, and instantly on receipt of this to send me a bit of your hair that I may have a consultation on it. Mind you, I don't want it for myself; I pledge you my word I'll burn it, or give you back every single hair. . . . but do if you please, mum, gratify my curiosity in this matter and consult the soothsayer regarding you. M. showed him letters, and vows he is right in every particular. And as I sha'n't be very long here I propose by return of post, for this favour.

Are you going to dine at Lansdowne House on Saturday? The post is come in and brought me an invitation, and a letter from my Ma, and my daughters, but none from my sister. Are you ill again, dear lady? Don't be ill, God bless you—good bye. I shall write again if you please, but I sha'n't be long before I come. Don't be ill, I am afraid you are. You hav'n't been to Kensington. My love to Mr. Williams, farewell, and write tomorrow.

1849.

[*To Mr. Brookfield*]

MY DEAR VIEUX:

If you come home in any decent time I wish you would go off to poor Mrs. Crowe at Hampstead.* A letter has just come, from Eugenie, who describes the poor lady as low, wretched, and hysterical—she may drop. Now a word or two of kindness from a black coat might make all the difference to her, and who so able to administer as your reverence? I am going out myself to laugh, talk and to the best of my ability, soothe and cheer her; but the professional man is the best, depend upon it, and I wish you would stretch a point in order to see her.

Yours till this evening.

[1849]

[*To Mr. Brookfield*]

MY DEAR VIEUX:

I wish you would go and call upon Lady Ashburton. Twice Ashburton has told me that she wants to make your acquaintance, and twice remarked that it would be but an act of politeness in you to call on a lady in distress, who wants your services. Both times I have said that you are uncommonly proud and shy, and last night told him he had best call on you, which he said he should hasten to do. But surely you might stretch a leg over the barrier when there's a lady actually beckoning to you to come over, and such an uncom-

---

* Mrs. Crowe, mother of Eyre Crowe, the well-known artist, who went with Mr. Thackeray to America on his first tour there, and who was always one of his most faithful friends.

monly good dinner laid on the other side. There was a vacant place yesterday, as you might have had, and such a company of jolly dogs, St. Davids, Hallam sen'r and ever so many more of our set. Do come if you can, and believe me to be yours,

A. PENDENNIS, MAJOR H.P.

To the Rev. W. H. Brookfield.

Monday.

MY DEAR VIEUX:

A. Sterling* dines with me at the Garrick at seven on Friday; I hope you will come too. And on Friday the 21st. June, Mr. Thackeray requests the pleasure of Mr. and Mrs. Brookfield's and Mr. Henry Hallam's company at dinner at 7.30 to meet Sir Alexander and Lady Duff Gordon, Sir Henry and Lady De Bathe &c. &c. I hope you will both come to this, please; you ought to acknowledge the kindness of the key,† and those kind Gordons will like to see you.

About 1849.

MY DEAR LADY:

A note comes asking me to dine tomorrow with *Mr. Benedict*,‡ close by you at No. 2 Manchester Square, to meet Mdme Jenny Lind. I reply that a lady is coming to dine with my mother, whom I must of course meet, but that I hope Mrs. B. will allow me to come to her in the evening with my mamma and this lady under each arm, and I promise they will

---
* A. Sterling, brother to John Sterling of whom Carlyle wrote the life.
† The key of the Portman Square Garden which was kindly lent to me.
‡ Mr. Benedict, the late lamented and kindly musician, Sir Julius Benedict.

look and behave well. Now suppose Mrs. S. and I were to come and dine with you, or my mother alone, if you liked to have her better; yes, that would be best, and I could come at nine o'clock and accompany you to the Swedish nightingale.

I am as usual
Your obedient servant
CLARENCE BULBUL.

[1849]

MY DEAR LADY:

It was begun, "dear Sir," to somebody of the other sex. I think it is just possible, that Mr. William on returning to-day, may like to have his wife to himself, and that the appearance of my eternal countenance might be a bore, hence I stay away. . . .

And about tomorrow, the birthday of my now motherless daughter, Miss Annie. Will you come out,—being as I must consider you, if you please, the children's aunt,—at two, or three o'clk, or so, and take innocent pleasures with them, such as the Coliseum and the Zoological Gardens? and are you free so as to give them some dinner or tea in the evening? I dine out myself at 8 o'clock, and should like them to share innocent pleasures with their relation.

My mother writes from Fareham that the old great aunt is better, and will not depart probably yet awhile.

And now concerning Monday. You two must please remember that you are engaged to this house at seven. I have written to remind the Scotts, to ask the Pollocks, and the Carlyles are coming.

And now with regard to this evening, I dine in Westbourne Terrace, then I must go to Marshall's in Eaton Square and then to Mrs. Sartoris, where I don't expect to see you; but if a gentleman of the name of W. H. B. should have a mind to come, we might &c. &c.

Madam, I hope you have had a pleasant walk on Clapham's breezy common, and that you are pretty well. I myself was very quiet, went with the children to Hampstead, and then to the Opera, and only one party. I am writing at the Reform Club, until four o'clock, when I have an engagement with O! such a charming person, and *tête-à-tête* too. Well, it's with the dentist's arm chair, but I should like to have the above queries satisfactorily answered, and am always Madam's

W. M. T.

13 July 1849

From Brighton.

Now for to go to begin that long letter which I have a right to send you, after keeping silence, or the next thing to silence, for a whole week. As I have nothing to tell about, it is the more likely to be longer and funnier—no, not funnier, for I believe I am generally most funny when I am most melancholy,—and who can be melancholy with such air, ocean and sunshine? not if I were going to be hanged tomorrow could I afford to be anything but exceedingly lazy, hungry and comfortable. Why is a day's Brighton the best of doctors? I don't mean this for a riddle, but I got up hungry, and have been yawning in the sun like a fat *lazzarone*, with great happiness all day. I have got a window with a magnificent prospect, a fresh sea breeze blowing in, such a blue sea yonder as can scarcely be beat by the Naples or the Mediterranean blue; and have passed the main part of the morning reading O! such a stupid book,

Fanny Hervey, the new *intime* novel of the season, as good as Miss Austen's people say. In two hours I am engaged to dinner in London. Well, I have broken with that place thank Heaven, for a little, and shall only go back to do my plates and to come away. Whither to go? I have a fancy that Ryde in the Isle of Wight would be as nice a place as any for idling, for sketching, for dawdling, and getting health; but the Rev. Mr. Brookfield must determine this for me, and I look to see him here in a day or two.

. . . I wish they had called me sooner to dinner; there's only one man staying at this house, and he asked me at breakfast in a piteous tone, to let him dine with me. If we were two, he said, the rules of the club would allow us a joint,—as if this luxury would tempt the voluptuary who pens these lines. He has come down here suffering from indigestion, and with a fatal dying look, which I have seen in one or two people before; he rushed wildly upon the joint and devoured it with famished eagerness. He said he had been curate of St. James, Westminster,—whereupon I asked if he knew my friend Brookfield. "My successor," says he, "a very able man, very good fellow, married a very nice woman." Upon my word he said all this, and of course it was not my business to contradict him. He said, no, he didn't say, but the waiter said, without my asking, that his name was Mr. Palmer; and then he asked if Brookfield had any children, so I said I believed not, and began to ask about his own children. How queer it seemed to be talking in this way, and what 2½d incidents to tell; but there are no others; nobody is here. The paper this morning announced the death of dear old Horace Smith,* that good serene old man, who went out of the world in charity with all in it, and having

---

* Horace Smith and his brother were the authors of "Rejected Addresses." The two Miss Horace Smiths are still living at Brighton, where Mr. Thackeray speaks of meeting them after his illness. Their society is still much sought after.

IN THE NURSERY AT CLEVEDON COURT

[From the Clevedon Drawings]

shown through his life, as far as I knew it, quite a delightful love of God's works and creatures,—a true, loyal, Christian man. So was Morier, of a different order, but possessing that precious natural quality of love, which is awarded to some lucky minds such as these, Charles Lambs, and one or two more in our trade; to many amongst the parsons I think; to a friend of yours by the name of Makepeace, perhaps, but not unalloyed to this one. O! God purify it, and make my heart clean. After dinner and a drive on the sea shore, I came home to an evening's reading which took place as follows—

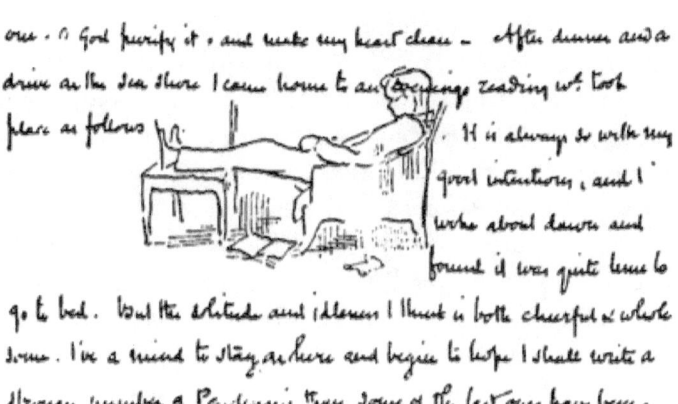

It is always so with my good intentions, and I woke about dawn, and found it was quite time to go to bed. But the solitude and idleness I think is both cheerful and wholesome. I've a mind to stay on here, and begin to hope I shall write a stronger number of Pendennis than some of the last ones have been. The Clevedon plan was abandoned before I came away; some place in S. Wales, I forget what, was fixed upon by the old folks. I would go with them, but one has neither the advantage of society nor of being alone, and it is best to follow my own ways. What a flood of egotism is being poured out on you! Well, I do think of some other people in the world besides myself.

. . . . . .

1849.

BRIGHTON, Saturday—Monday.

Thank you for your letter, dear Mrs. Brookfield; it made this gay place look twice as gay yesterday when I got it. Last night when I had come home to work, two men spied a light in my room, and came in and began smoking. They talked about racing and the odds all the time. One of them I am happy to say is a lord, and the other a Brighton buck. When they were gone (and indeed I listened to them with a great deal of pleasure for I like to hear people of all sorts,) at mid-night, and in the quiet I read your letter over again, and one from Miss Annie, and from my dear old mother, who is to come on the 12th. and whose heart is yearning for her children. I must be at home to receive her, and some days, ten or so at least, to make her comfortable, so with many thanks for Mrs. Elton's invitation, I must decline it for the present if you please. You may be sure I went the very first thing to Virginia and her sisters, who were very kind to me, and I think are very fond of me, and their talk and beauty consoled me, for my heart was very sore and I was ill and out of spirits. A change, a fine air, a wonderful sunshine and moonlight, and a great Spectacle of happy people perpetually rolling by, has done me all the good in the world, and then one of the Miss Smiths* told me a story which is the very thing for the beginning of Pendennis, which is actually begun and in progress. This is a comical beginning rather. The other, which I didn't like was sentimental, and will yet come in very well after the startling comical business has been played off. See how beautifully I have put stops to the last sentence, and crossed the t's and dotted the i's! It was written four hours ago, before dinner, before Jullien's concert, before a walk by the sea shore.—I have been thinking what a number of ladies, and gentlemen too, live like you just now, in a smart papered rooms, with rats gnawing behind the wainscot; Be hanged to the rats, but they are a sort of company. You must have a poker ready, and if the rats come out, *bang!* beat them on the head. This is an allegory, why, it would work up into a little moral poem if you chose to write it. Jullien was splendid in his white waistcoat, and played famous easy music which anybody may comprehend and like. There was a delightful cornet à piston, (mark the accent on the a). The fact is I am thinking about something else all the while and am very tired and weary, but I thought I would like to say good night to you, and what news shall I give you just for the last? Well then, Miss Virginia is gone away, not to come back while I am here. Good night, ma'am, if you please.

. . . Being entirely occupied with my two new friends, Mrs. Pendennis and her son Mr. Arthur Pendennis, I got up very early again this morning, and was with them for more than two hours before breakfast. He is a very good natured

---

* The Miss Smiths here referred to are the daughters of the late Horace Smith, author of "Rejected Addresses."

The Virginia here mentioned was the beautiful Miss Pattle, then in her earliest youth, and who is now the widow of the late Earl Somers. In those days she lived with her sister and her husband, Mr. and Mrs. Thoby Prinsep at Little Holland House, Kensington, where they gathered around them a charming society and where Mr. Thackeray was ever welcomed, almost as one of the family. Their garden parties will ever be remembered.

generous young fellow, and I begin to like him considerably. I wonder whether he is interesting to me from selfish reasons and because I fancy we resemble each other in many points, and whether I can get the public to like him too? We had the most magnificent sunshine Sunday, and I passed the evening very rationally with Mr. Fonblanque and Mr. Sheil, a great orator of whom perhaps you have heard, at present lying here afflicted with gout, and with such an Irish wife. Never was a truer saying than that those people are foreigners. They have neither English notions, manners, nor morals. I mean what is right and natural to them, is absurd and unreasonable to us. It was as good as Mrs. O'Dowd to hear Mrs. Sheil interrupt her Richard and give her opinions on the state of Ireland, to those two great, hard-headed, keen, accomplished men of the world. Richard listened to her foolishness with admirable forbearance and good humour. I am afraid I don't respect your sex enough, though. Yes I do, when they are occupied with loving and sentiment rather than with other business of life.

I had a mind to send you a weekly paper containing contemptuous remarks regarding an author of your acquaintance. I don't know who this critic is, but he always has a shot at me once a month, and I bet a guinea he is an Irishman.

So we have got the cholera. Are you looking out for a visit? Did you try the Stethoscope, and after listening at your chest, did it say that your lungs were sore?

Fragment.

[1849.]

I am going to dine at the Berrys to-day and to Lady Ashburton's at night. I dined at home three days running, think of that. This is my news, it isn't much is it? I have written a wicked number of *Pendennis*, but like it rather, it has a good moral, I believe, although to some it may appear naughty. Big Higgins * who dined with me yesterday offered me, what do you think? " If" says he, " you are tired and want to lie fallow for a year, come to me for the money. I have much more than I want." Wasn't it kind? I like to hear and to tell of kind things.

Wednesday. 1849.

What have I been doing since these many days? I hardly know. I have written such a stupid number of *Pendennis* in consequence of not seeing you, that I shall be ruined if you are to stay away much longer. . . . Has William written to you about our trip to Hampstead on Sunday? It was very pleasant. We went first to St. Mark's church, where I always thought you went, but where the pew opener had never heard of such a person as Mrs. J. O. B.; and having heard a jolly and perfectly stupid sermon, walked over Primrose Hill to the Crowes', where His Reverence gave Mrs. Crowe half an hour's private talk, whilst I was talking under the blossoming apple tree about newspapers to Monsieur Crowe. Well, Mrs. Crowe was delighted with William and his manner of *discoorsing* her; and indeed though I say it

* Big Higgins—the well-known writer under the signature of Jacob Omnium.

that shouldn't, from what he said afterwards, and from what we have often talked over pipes in private, that is a pious and kind soul. I mean his, and calculated to soothe and comfort and appreciate and elevate so to speak out of despair, many a soul that your more tremendous, rigorous divines would leave on the way side, where sin, that robber, had left them half killed. I will have a Samaritan parson when I fall among thieves. You, dear lady, may send for an ascetic if you like; what is he to find wrong in you?

I have talked to my mother about her going to Paris with the children, she is very much pleased at the notion, and it won't be very lonely to me. I shall be alone for some months at any rate, and vow and swear I'll save money. . . . Have you read Dickens? O! it is charming! brave Dickens! It has some of his very prettiest touches—those inimitable Dickens touches which make such a great man of him; and the reading of the book has done another author a great deal of good. In the first place it pleases the other author to see that Dickens, who has long left off alluding to the A.'s works, has been copying the O. A., and greatly simplifying his style, and overcoming the use of fine words. By this the public will be the gainer and *David Copperfield* will be improved by taking a lesson from *Vanity Fair*. Secondly it has put me upon my metal; for ah! Madame, all the metal was out of me and I have been dreadfully and curiously cast down this month past. I say, secondly, it has put me on my metal and made me feel I must do something; that I have fame and name and family to support. . . .

I have just come away from a dismal sight; Gore House full of snobs looking at the furniture. Foul Jews; odious bombazine women, who drove up in mysterious flys which they had hired, the wretches, to be fined, so as to come in state to a fashionable lounge; brutes keeping their hats on in the kind old drawing room,—I longed to knock some of

CLEVEDON CHURCH

them off, and say " Sir, be civil in a lady's room." . . .
There was one of the servants there, not a powdered one,
but a butler, a *whatdyoucallit*. My heart melted towards him
and I gave him a pound, Ah! it was a strange, sad picture
of *Vanity Fair*. My mind is all boiling up with it; indeed,
it is in a queer state. .   . I give my best remembrances
to all at Clevedon Court.

[30th *June* 1849.]

MY DEAR LADY:

I have 2 opera boxes for tonight—a pit box—for the Huguenots at Covent Garden—where there is no ballet, and where you might sit and see this grand opera in great ease and quiet. Will you please to say if you will have it and I will send or bring it.

Or if Miss Hallam dines with you, may I come afterwards to tea? Say yes or no; I sha'n't be offended, only best pleased of course with yes. I am engaged on Monday Tuesday and Wednesday nights, so if you go away on Thursday I shall have no chance of seeing you again for ever so long.

I was to breakfast with Mr. Rogers this morning but he played me false.

Good bye
W. M. T.

Fragment.

21 July 1849.

[*To Mr. Brookfield.*]

Adelaide Procter has sent me the most elegant velvet purse, embroidered with my initials, and forget-me-nots on the other side. I received this peace-offering with a gentle heart; one must not lose old friends at our time of life, and if one has offended them one must try and try until they are brought back. . . .

Mrs. Powell, the lady I asked you to stir about, has got the place of matron of the Governesses, a house and perquisites, and 100 a year, an immense thing for a woman with nothing.

On the 30th June, the day you went, Rogers threw me over for breakfast, and to-day comes the most lamentable letter of excuse. Yesterday, the day madame went away, the Strutts asked me to Greenwich, and when I got there, no dinner. Another most pathetic letter of excuse. These must be answered in a witty manner, so must Miss Procter, for the purse; so must Mrs. Alfred Montgomery, who offers a dinner on Monday; so must two more, and I must write that *demnition* Mr. Browne before evensong.

From the *Punch* office, where I'm come for to go to dress, to dine with the Lord mayor; but I have nothing to say but that I am yours, my dear old friend, affectionately,

W. M. T.

Fragment.

[1849]

I was to go to Mrs. Montgomery's at this hour of 10.30, but it must be the contrary, that is, Mrs. Procter's. I wrote Adelaide her letter for the purse, and instead of thanking her much, only discoursed about old age, disappointment, death, and melancholy.

The old people are charming at home, with their kindness. They are going away at the end of the week, somewhere, they don't say where, with the children. The dear old step-father moves me rather the most, he is so gentle and good humoured. Last night Harry came to dinner, and being Sunday there was none, and none to be had, and we went to the tavern hard-bye, where he didn't eat a bit. I did. . . . .

At Procter's was not furiously amusing—the eternal G. bores one. Her parents were of course there, the papa with a suspicious looking little order in his button hole, and a *chevalier d'industrie* air, which I can't get over. E. didn't sing, but on the other hand Mrs. —— did. She was passionate, she was enthusiastic, she was sublime, she was tender. There was one note that she kept so long, that I protest I had time to think about my affairs, to have a little nap, and to awake much refreshed, while it was going on still. At another time, overcome by almost unutterable tenderness, she piped so low, that it's a wonder one could hear at all. In a word, she was *mirobolante*, the most artless, affected, good-natured, absurd, clever creature possible. When she had crushed G. who stood by the piano hating her, and paying her the most profound compliments—she tripped off on my arm to the cab in waiting. I like that absurd kind creature.

Drums are beating in various quarters for parties yet to come off, but I am refusing any more, being quite done up. I am thinking of sending the old and young folks to Clevedon, I am sure Mrs. Robbins and Mrs. Parr will be kind to them, won't they?

[During an Illness, August 1849]

No. 1.

63 East Street, Brighton.

Yesterday I had the courage to fly to Brighton, I have got a most beautiful lodging, and had a delightful sleep. I write a line at seven o'clock of the morning to tell you these good news. G b y.—

No. 2.

63 East Street Brighton.

This morning's, you know, wasn't a letter, only to tell you that I was pretty well after my travels; and after the letter was gone, thinks I, the handwriting is so bad and shaky, she will think I am worse, and only write fibs to try and soothe her. But the cause of the bad writing was a bad pen, and impossible ink. See how different this is, though I have not much to say now, only that I have been sitting on the chain pier in a bath chair for two hours, and feel greatly invigorated and pleasantly tired by the wholesome sea breezes. Shall I be asleep in two minutes I wonder? I think I will try, I think snoring is better than writing. Come,

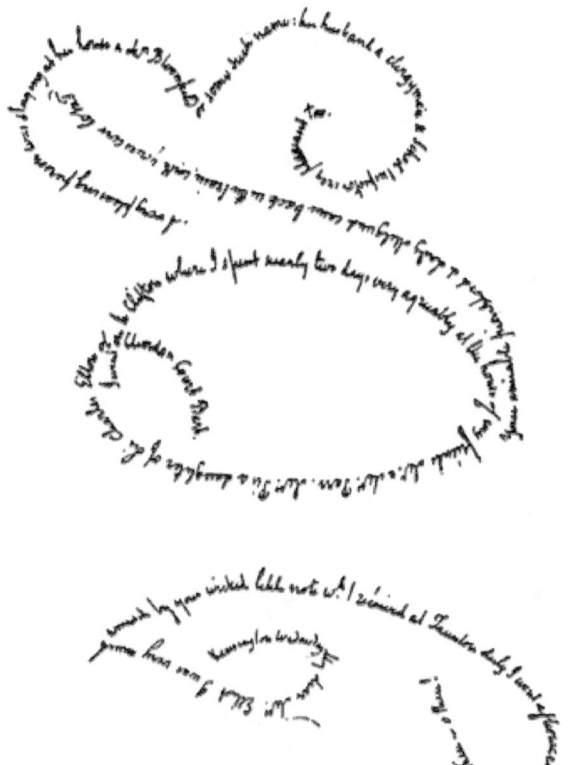

[Note sent by Thackeray to Mrs. Elliot.]

KENSINGTON, Wednesday.

MY DEAR MRS. ELLIOT,

I was very much amused by your wicked little note, which I received at Taunton duly. I went elsewhere, to Lady A. Shaw's there! I went on to a house where I spent nearly ten days very agreeably at the house of my friends Mr. & Mrs. Fart. Mrs. F. is a daughter of our Charles Elton of Clevedon Court Park. A very pleasant person at her house. A Mrs. Bland—kind I dont know such name: her husband a clergyman came back in the train with pretty poem. I saw amiable friends Lord and Lady McLeod, and back in the train with poets ever

W. M. T.

let us try a little doze ; a comfortable little doze of a quarter of an hour.

Since then, a somewhat fatiguing visit from the Miss Smiths, who are all kindness, and look very pretty in their mourning.* I found acquaintances on the pier too, and my chair anchored alongside of that of a very interesting nice little woman, Mrs. Whitmore, so that there was more talkee-talkee. Well, I won't go on writing any more about my ailments, and dozes and fatigues ; but sick folks are abominably selfish ; sick men that is, and so God bless my dear lady.

W. M. T.

Thursday.

I cannot write you long, dear lady ; I have two notes to my mother daily, and a long one to Elliotson, &c. ; but I am getting on *doucement*, like the change of air exceedingly, the salt water baths, and the bath-chair journeys to the pier where it is almost as fresh as being at sea. But do you go on writing, please, and as often as you can ; for it does me good to get kind letters. God bless you and good-night, is all I can say now, with my love to his Reverence from

W. M. T.

* Horace Smith died 12th July, 1849.

[*Paris, Feb.* 1849]

My dear Lady:

I have been to see a great character to-day and another still greater yesterday. To-day was Jules Janin, whose books you never read, nor do I suppose you could very well. He is the critic of the Journal des Débats and has made his weekly feuilleton famous throughout Europe—He does not know a word of English, but he translated Sterne and I think Clarissa Harlowe. One week, having no theatres to describe in his feuilleton, or no other subject handy, he described his own marriage, which took place in fact that week, and absolutely made a present of his sensations to all the European public. He has the most wonderful verve, humour, oddity, honesty, bonhomie. He was ill with the gout, or recovering perhaps; but bounced about the room, gesticulating, joking, gasconading, quoting Latin, pulling out his books which are very handsome, and tossing about his curling brown hair;— a magnificent jolly intelligent face such as would suit Pan I should think, a flood of humourous, rich, jovial talk. And now I have described this, how are you to have the least idea of him.—I daresay it is not a bit like him. He recommended me to read Diderot; which I have been reading in at his recommendation; and that is a remarkable sentimental cynic, too; in his way of thinking and sudden humours not unlike —not unlike Mr. Bowes of the Chatteris Theatre. I can fancy Harry Pendennis and him seated on the bridge and talking of their mutual mishaps;—no Arthur Pendennis the boy's name is! I shall be forgetting my own next. But mind you, my similes don't go any further: and I hope you don't go for to fancy that you know anybody like Miss Fotheringay—you don't suppose that I think that you have no heart, do you? But there's many a woman who has none.

and about whom men go crazy;—such was the other character I saw yesterday. We had a long talk in which she showed me her interior, and I inspected it and left it in a state of wonderment which I can't describe. . . .

She is kind, frank, open-handed, not very refined, with a warm outpouring of language; and thinks herself the most feeling creature in the world. The way in which she fascinates some people is quite extraordinary. She affected me by telling me of an old friend of ours in the country—Dr. Portman's daughter indeed, who was a parson in our parts—who died of consumption the other day after leading the purest and saintliest life, and who after she had received the sacrament read over her friend's letter and actually died with it on the bed. Her husband adores her; he is an old cavalry Colonel of sixty, and the poor fellow away now in India, and yearning after her writes her yards and yards of the most tender, submissive, frantic letters; five or six other men are crazy about her. She trotted them all out, one after another before me last night; not humourously, I mean, nor making fun of them; but complacently, describing their adoration for her and acquiescing in their opinion of herself. Friends, lover, husband, she coaxes them all; and no more cares for them than worthy Miss Fotheringay did.—Oh! Becky is a trifle to her; and I am sure I might draw her picture and she would never know in the least that it was herself. I suppose I did not fall in love with her myself because we were brought up together; she was a very simple generous creature then.

Tuesday. Friend came in as I was writing last night, perhaps in time to stop my chattering; but I am *encore tout émerveillé de ma cousine.* By all the Gods! I never had the opportunity of inspecting such a naturalness and coquetry; not that I suppose that there are not many such women; but I have only myself known one or two women intimately, and I daresay the novelty would wear off if I knew more. I had the *Revue des 2 mondes* and the *Journal des Débats* to dinner; and what do you think by way of a delicate attention the *chef* served us up? Mock-turtle soup again, and uncommonly good it was too. After dinner I went to a ball at the prefecture of Police; the most splendid apartments I ever saw in my life. Such lights, pillars, marble, hangings, carvings, and gildings. I am sure King Belshazzar could not have been more magnificently lodged.— There must have been 15 hundred people, of whom I did not know one single soul. I am surprised that the people did not faint in the Saloons, which were like burning fiery furnaces; but there they were dancing and tripping away, ogling and flirting, and I suppose not finding the place a bit inconveniently warm. The women were very queer looking bodies for the most, I thought, but the men dandies every one, fierce and trim with curling little mustachios. I felt dimly that I was 3 inches taller than any body else in the room but I hoped that nobody took notice of me. There was a rush for ices at a footman who brought those refreshments which was perfectly terrific.—They were scattered melting over the heads of the crowd, as I ran out of it in a panic. There was an old British dowager with two daughters seated up against a wall very dowdy and sad, poor old lady; I wonder what she wanted there and whether that was what she called pleasure. I went to see William's old friend and mine, Bowes; he has forty thousand a year and palaces in the country, and here he is a manager of a Theatre of Variétés, and his talk was about actors and coulisses all the time of our interview. I wish it could be the last, but he has made me promise to dine with him, and go I must, to be killed by his melancholy gentlemanlikeness. I think that is all I did yesterday. Dear lady, I am pained at your having been unwell; I thought you must have been, when Saturday came without any letter. There wont be one today I bet twopence. I am going to a lecture at the Institute; a lecture on Burns by M. Chasles, who is professor of English literature. What a course of lionizing, isn't it? But it must stop; for is not the month the shortest of months? I went to see my old haunts when I came to Paris 13 years ago, and made believe to be a painter,—just after I was ruined and before I fell in love and took to marriage and writing. It was a very jolly time, I was as poor as Job and sketched away most abominably, but pretty contented; and we used to meet in each others little rooms and talk about art and smoke pipes and drink bad brandy and water.—That awful habit still remains, but where is art, that dear mistress whom I loved, though in a very indolent capricious manner, but with a real sincerity?—I see her far, very far off. I jilted her, I know it very well; but you see it was Fate ordained *that* marriage should never take place; and forced me to take on with another lady, two other ladies, three other ladies; I mean the muse and my wife &c. &c.

Well you are very good to listen to all this egotistic prattle, chère soeur, si douce et si bonne. I have no reason to be ashamed of my loves, seeing that all three are quite lawful. Did you go to see my people yesterday? Some day when his reverence is away, will you have the children? and not, if you please, be so vain as to fancy that you can't amuse them or that they will be bored in your house. They must and shall be fond of you, if you please. Alfred's open mouth as he looked at the broken bottle and spilt wine must have been a grand picture of agony.

I couldn't find the lecture room at the Institute, so I went to the Louvre instead, and took a feast with the statues and pictures. The Venus of Milo is the grandest figure of figures. The wave of the lines of the figure, whenever seen, fills my senses with pleasure. What is it which so charms, satisfies one, in certain lines? O! the man who achieved that statue was a beautiful genius. I have been sitting thinking of it these 10 minutes in a delightful sensuous rumination. The Colours of the Titian pictures comfort one's eyes similarly; and after these feasts, which wouldn't please my lady very much I daresay, being I should think too earthly for you, I went and looked at a picture I usedn't to care much for in old days, an angel saluting a Virgin and child by Pietro Cortona, —a sweet smiling angel with a lily in her hands, looking so tender and gentle I wished that instant to make a copy of it, and do it beautifully, which I cant, and present it to somebody on Lady-day.—There now, just fancy it is done, and presented in a neat compliment, and hung up in your room —a pretty piece—dainty and devotional?—I drove about with——, and wondered at her more and more.—She is come to "my dearest William" now: though she doesn't care a fig for me.—She told me astonishing things, showed me a letter in which every word was true and which was a fib from beginning to end;—A miracle of deception;—flattered, fondled, coaxed—O! she was worth coming to Paris for! . . . Pray God to keep us simple. I have never looked at anything in my life which has so amazed me. Why, this is as good, almost, as if I had you to talk to. Let us go out and have another walk.

Fragment

[*Paris*, 1849]

Of course in all families the mother is the one to whom the children cling. We don't talk to them, feel with them, love them, occupy ourselves about them as the female does. —We think about our business and pleasure, not theirs. Why do I trouble you with these perplexities? If I mayn't tell you what I feel, what is the use of a friend? That's why I would rather have a sad letter from you, or a short one if you are tired and unwell, than a sham-gay one—and I don't subscribe at all to the doctrine of " striving to be cheerful ". *À quoi bon*, convulsive grins and humbugging good-humour? Let us have a reasonable cheerfulness, and melancholy too, if there is occasion for it—and no more hypocrisy in life than need be.

We had a pleasant enough visit to Versailles, and then I went to see old Halliday, and then to see old Bess, and to sit with the sick Tom Fraser. I spend my days so, and upon my word ought to get some reward for being so virtuous.

On Sunday I took a carriage and went to S. in the country. The jolly old nurse who has been in the Ricketts family 120 years or more or less, talked about Miss Rosa, late Mrs Fanshawe, and remembers her the flower of that branch of the family, and exceedingly pretty and with a most lovely complexion.—And then I told them what a lovely jewel the present Miss Rosa was; and how very fond I was of her mamma; —and so we had a tolerably pleasant afternoon;—and I came back and sat again with Mr. Thomas Fraser. Yesterday there was a pretty little English dance next door at Mrs. Errington's, and an English country dance being proposed, one of the young bucks good-naturedly took a fiddle and played very well too, and I had for a partner Madame Gudin, the painters wife, I think I mentioned her to you, didn't I?

She is a daughter of Lord James Hay—a very fair complexion and jolly face, and so with the greatest fear and trepidation (for I never could understand a figure) I asked her—and she refused because she tells me that she is too ill, and I am sure I was very glad to be out of the business.

I went to see a play last night, and the new comedian Mademoiselle Brohan of whom all the world is talking, a beautiful young woman of 17 looking 25 and—I thought—vulgar, intensely affected, and with a kind of stupid intelligence that passes for real wit with the pittites, who applauded with immense enthusiasm all her smiles and shrugs and gestures and ogles. But they wouldn't have admired her if she hadn't been so beautiful, if her eyes weren't bright and her charms undeniable.—I was asked to beg some of the young English Seigneurs here to go to an Actress ball, where there was to be a great deal of Parisian beauty, which a cosmophilite ought to see perhaps as well as any other phase of society.—But I refused Madame Osy's ball—my grey head has no call to show amongst these young ones, and, as in the next novel we are to have none but good characters—what is the use of examining folks who are quite otherwise. Meanwhile, and for 10 days more, I must do my duty and go out feeling deucedly lonely in the midst of the racketting and jigging. I am engaged to dinner for the next 3 days, and on Friday when I had hoped to be at home—my mother has a tea-party, and asked trembling (for she is awfully afraid of me) whether I would come—Of course I'll go. — —

W. M. T.

Sunday 2 Sep^r.

Madam: letter made a very agreeable appearance upon the breakfast table this morning when I entered that apartment at 11 o'clock. I don't know how I can ag^d to sleep so much, but such was the fact. After a fine broiling hot day, utter idleness part of wch was spent on the sofa, a little in the Twillery gardens where I made a sketch that's not a masterpiece but p'raps Madam will like to see it: and the evening very merrily with the Morning Chronicle the Journal des Debats and Jules Janin at a jolly little Restaurateur's in the Champs Elysées at the Sign of the Petit Moulin Rouge. We had a private room & drank small wine very gaily looking out into a garden full of green arbours, in almost every one of wch were gentlemen & ladies in couples come to dine au frais, and afterwards to go & dance at the neighbouring dancing garden of Mabille. Fiddlers and singers came and performed for us: and who knows I should have gone to Mabille too, but there came down a tremendous thunder-storm with flashes of lightning to illuminate it, wch sent the little couples out of the arbours, and put out all the lights of Mabille. The day before I passed with my Aunt & cousins, who are not so pretty as some members of the family; but are dear good people with a fine sense of fun and we were very happy until the arrival of two newly-married Snobs, whose happiness disgusted me and drove me home early, to find 3 acquaintances smoking in the moonlight at the hotel door, who came up and passed the night in my rooms — No I forgot, I went to the play first: but only for an hour I couldn't stand more than an hour of the farce w: made me laugh while it lasted, but left a profound black melancholy behind it. Jamin said last night that life was the greatest of pleasures to him, that every morning when he woke he was thankful to be alive (this is very tolerably like him)

that he was always entirely happy, and had never known any such thing as blue devils or repentance or satiety. I had great fun giving him authentic

anecdotes of London. I told him that to see the people boxing in the streets was a constant source of amusement to us; that in November — you saw every lamp post on London Bridge with a man hanging from it who had committed suicide — and he believed everything. Did you ever read any of the works of

Janin? – No? Well he has been for 20 years famous in France: and he on his side has never heard of the works of Titmarsh, nor has anybody else here and that is a comfort.   I have got very nice rooms but they cost 10 francs a day: and I began in a dignified manner with a domestique de place, but sent him away after two days; for the idea that he was in the ante-room ceaselessly with nothing to do, made my life in my own room intolerable, and now I actually take my own letters to the post. I went to the Exhibition, it was full of portraits of the most hideous women, with unconceivable spots on their faces of wh. I think I've told you my horror; and scarcely 6 decent pictures in the whole enormous collection: but I had never been in the Tuilleries before, and it was curious to go through the vast dingy rooms by wh. such a number of dynasties have come in & gone out – Louis XVI, Napoleon, Charles X, Louis Philippe have all marched in state up the stairs case with the gilt balustrades, and come tumbling down again presently. – Well I won't give you an historical disquisition in the Titmarsh manner upon this but reserve it for Punch – for whom on Thursday an article that I think is quite unexampled for dullness even in that Journal, and that beats the dullest Jerrold. What a jaunty off hand Saturnic rogue I am to be sure - and a gay young dog-! I took a very great liking and admiration for Clough. He is a real poet and a simple affectionate creature. Last year we went to Blenheim from Oxford (it was after a stay at Cl-ved-n C-t the seat of Sir C— E—n B-t) and I liked him for setting down in the Inn yard and beginning to teach a child to read off a bit of French wh. was lying on the ground - Subsequently he sent me his poems wh. were rough but contain the real genuine sacred flame I think. He is very learned; he has evidently been crossed in love: he gave up his fellowship and university prospects on religious scruples. He is one of those thinking men, who I daresay will begin to speak out before many years are over, and protest against Gothic Xtianity. - That is I think he is - Did you read in J. Newman's book? There speaks a very pious loving humble Soul I think, with an ascetical continence too - and a beautiful love and reverence - I'm a publican and sinner; but I believe these men are on the true track

[*Paris*, 1849]

They all got a great shock they told me, by reading in the *Galignani*, that W. M. Thackeray was dead, and that it was I. Indeed two W. Thackeray's have died within the last month. *Eh bien?* There's a glum sort of humour in all this I think, and I grin like a skull.—As I sent you a letter to my Mamma, here is a sermon to Annie. You will please put it in the post for me? I think about my dear honest old Fatty, with the greatest regard and confidence. I hope, please God, she will be kept to be a companion and friend to me. You see I work in the Herschell.

Give my love to Harry when you write to him, and to Mrs. Fanshawe and to Missy. I haven't time to transact letters to them to-day, or I should use our traveller who carries this here, and glory in saving 2*f.* by that stratagem. And I'd have you know, Madam, that I wish I was going to dine at Portman Street as I did this day week; but that as I can't, why, I will be a man, and do my duty. *Bon soir* William, *bon soir Madame.*

A Fragment

[1849]

What you say about Mrs. —— being doomed does not affect me very much, I am afraid. I don't see that living is such a benefit, and could find it in my heart pretty readily to have an end of it,—After wasting a deal of opportunities and time and desires in vanitarianism. What is it makes one so blasé and tired I wonder at 38? Is it pain or pleasure?

Present solitude or too much company before? both very likely. You see I am here as yesterday, gloomy again, and thrumming on the old egotistical string.—But that I think you would be pleased to have a letter from me dear lady, I'd burn these 2 sheets, or give my blue devils some other outlet than into your kind heart.

Here are some verses which I have been knocking about, and are of the same gloomy tendency. You must know that I was making a drawing which was something like you at first, but ended in a face that is not in the least like yours; whereupon the Poet ever on the watch for incidents began A Failure.

A Failure

Beneath this frank and smiling face,
    You who would look with curious eye
    The draughtsman's inward mind to spy,
Some other lineaments may trace.
    Ah! many a time I try and try
Lady, to represent their grace.

Dear face! The smile with which 'tis lit
    The mantling blush, the gentle eyes,
    Each individual feature lies
Within my heart so faithful writ.
    Why fails my pencil when it tries?

   .   .   .   .   .

(Here lines may be inserted *Ad lib.* complimentary to the person)

Ye flags of Piccadilly,
Which I hated once, I vow
I could wish with all my soul
You were underneath me now,

[From the original manuscript of Clough's "Flags of Piccadilly," with a drawing by Thackeray, in the possession of Mr. James Russell Lowell.]

I look upon the altered line
　And think it ever is my lot;
　A something always comes to blot
And mar my impossible design—
A mocking Fate that bids me pine,
　And struggle and achieve it not.

Poor baulked endeavours incomplete!
　Poor feeble sketch the world to show,
　While the marred truth lurks lost below!
What's life but this? a cancelled sheet,
A laugh disguising a defeat!
　Let's tear and laugh and own it so.

> Exit with a laugh of demoniac scorn. But I send the very original drawing, to these very original verses—

3 Sept. 1849.

From Paris,
Monday.

The man who was to carry my letter yesterday, fled without giving me notice, so Madame loses the sermon to Annie, the pretty picture, &c. I haven't the courage to pay the postage for so much rubbish. Isn't it curious that a gentleman of such expensive habits should have this meanness about paper and postage? The best is that I have spent three francs in cab-hire, hunting for the man who was to carry my two-franc letter. The follies of men are ceaseless, even of comic authors, who make it their business to laug hat the follies of all the rest of the world.

What do you think I did yesterday night? If you please, ma'am, I went to the play; and I suppose because it was Sunday, was especially diverted, and laughed so as to make myself an object in the stalls; but it was at pure farcicality, not at wit. The piece was about a pleasure excursion to London; and the blunders and buffoonery, mingled, made the laughter. "*Eh oui, nous irons à Greenwich, manger un excellent sandwich*" was a part of one of the songs.

My poor Aunt is still in life, but that is all; she has quite lost her senses. I talked for some time with her old husband, who has been the most affectionate husband to her, and who is looking on, he being 72 years old himself, with a calm resolution and awaiting the moment which is to take away his life's companion. . . . As for Pendennis, I began upon No. 7 to-day and found a picture which was perfectly new and a passage which I had as utterly forgotten as if I had never read or written it. This shortness of memory frightens me, and makes me have gloomy anticipations. Will poor Annie have to nurse an old imbecile of a father some day, who will ramble incoherently about old days and people whom he used to love? What a shame it is to talk such gloomy stuff to my dear lady; well, you are accustomed to hear my chatter, gloomy or otherwise, as my thoughts go by. I fancy myself by the dear old sofa almost, as I sit here prating; and shut my eyes and see you quite clear. I am glad you have been doing works of art with your needle. . . .

W. H. Ainsworth, Esquire, is here; we dined next each other at the *3 Frères* yesterday and rather fraternized. He showed a friendly disposition I thought, and a desire to forgive me my success; but beyond a good-humoured acquiescence in his good will, I don't care. I suppose one doesn't care for people, only for a very, very few. A man came in just now who told me he had heard how I was dead. I began to laugh, and my laugh meant, "Well old fellow, you don't care, do you?" And why should he? How often I must have said and said these things over to you. *Oui Madame, je me répète. Je me fais vieux; j'oublie; je radote; je ne parle que de moi. Je vous fais subir mon égoisme, ma mélancholie. —Le jour viendra-t-il où elle vous gênera? Eh, mon dieu; —ne soyons pas trop curieux; demain viendra; aujourd' hui j'oublierai—pourquoi ne vous vois-je pas aujour-d' hui?* I think you have enough of this for to-day, so good-night. Good bye, Mr. Williams. I fancy the old street-sweeper at the corner is holding the cob, I take my hat and stick, I say good bye again, the door bangs finally. Here's a shilling for you, old street-sweeper; the cob trots solitary into the Park. *Je fais de la littérature, ma parole d'honneur!—du style— du Sterne tout pur—O vanitas vanitatum!* God bless all,

W. M. T.

[*4th Sept.* 1849]

TUESDAY, PARIS.

Perhaps by my intolerable meanness and blundering, you will not get any letter from me till to-morrow. On Sunday, the man who was to take the letter failed me; yesterday I went with it in a cab to the Grande Poste, which is a mile off, and where you have to go to pay. The cab horse was lame, and we arrived two minutes too late; I put the letter into the unpaid-letter box; I dismissed the poor old broken cab horse, behind which it was agonizing to sit; in fine it was a failure.

When I got to dinner at my aunt's, I found all was over. Mrs. H. died on Sunday night in her sleep, quite without pain, or any knowledge of the transition. I went and sat with her husband, an old fellow of seventy-two, and found him bearing his calamity in a very honest manly way. What do you think the old gentleman was doing? Well, he was drinking gin and water, and I had some too, telling his valet to make me some. Man thought this was a master-stroke of diplomacy and evidently thinks I have arrived to take possession as heir, but I know nothing about money matters as yet, and think that the old gentleman at least will have the enjoyment of my aunt's property during life. He told me some family secrets, in which persons of repute figure not honorably. Ah! they shock one to think of. Pray, have you ever committed any roguery in money matters? Has William? Have I? I am more likely to do it than he, that honest man, not having his resolution or self-denial. But I've not as yet, beyond the roguery of not saving perhaps, which is knavish too. I am very glad I came to see my dearest old aunt. She is such a kind tender creature, laws bless us, how fond she would be of you. I was going to begin about William and say, 'do you remember a friend of mine who came to dine at the Thermes, and sang the song about the Mogul, and the blue-bottle fly,' but modesty forbade and I was dumb.

Since this was written in the afternoon I suppose if there has been one virtuous man in Paris it is madame's most *obajient* servant. I went to sit with Mr. H. and found him taking what he calls his tiffin in great comfort (tiffin is the meal which I have sometimes had the honor of sharing with you at one o'clock) and this transacted,—and I didn't have any tiffin, having consumed a good breakfast two hours previously —I went up a hundred stairs at least, to Miss. B. H.'s airy apartment, and found her and her sister, and sat for an hour. She asked after you so warmly that I was quite pleased; she said she had the highest respect for you, and I was glad to find somebody who knew you; and all I can say is, if you fancy I like being here better than in London, you are in a pleasing error;

Then I went to see a friend of my mother's, then to have a very good dinner at the Café de Paris, where I had *potage à la pourpart*, think of *pourpart* soup. We had it merely for the sake of the name, and it was uncommonly good. Then back to old H. again, to bawl into his ears for an hour and a half; then to drink tea with my aunt—why, life has been a series of sacrifices today, and I must be written up in the book of good works. For I should have liked to go to the play, and follow my own devices best, but for that stern sentiment of duty, which fitfully comes over the most abandoned of men, at times. All the time I was with Mr. H. in the morning, what do you think they were doing in the next room? It was like a novel. They were rapping at a coffin in the bedroom, but he was too deaf to hear, and seems too old to care very much. Ah! dear lady, I hope you are sleeping happily at this hour, and you, and Mr. Williams, and another party who is nameless, shall have all the benefits of an old sinner's prayers.

I suppose I was too virtuous on Tuesday, for yesterday I got back to my old selfish ways again, and did what I liked from morning till night. This self indulgence though entire was not criminal, at first at least, but I shall come to the painful part of my memoirs presently. All the forenoon I read with intense delight, a novel called *Le Vicomte de Bragelonne*, a continuation of the famous *Mousquetaires* and just as interesting, keeping one panting from volume to volume, and longing for more. This done, and after a walk and some visits, read more novels, *David Copperfield* to wit, in which there is a charming bit of insanity, and which I begin to believe is the very best thing the author has yet done. Then to the *Variétés* Theatre, to see the play *Chaméléon*, after which all Paris is running, a general satire upon the last 60 years. Everything is satirised, Louis XVI, the Convention, the Empire, the Restoration etc., the barricades, at which these people were murdering each other only yesterday—it's awful, immodest, surpasses my cynicism altogether. At the end of the piece they pretend to bring in the author and a little child who can just speak, comes in and sings a satiric song, in a feeble, tender, infantine pipe, which seemed to me as impious as the whole of the rest of the piece. They don't care for anything, not religion, not bravery, not liberty, not great men, not modesty. Ah! madame, what a great moralist somebody is, and what *moighty foine* principles *entoirely* he has!

But now, with a blush upon my damask cheek, I come to the adventures of the day. You must know I went to the play with an old comrade, Roger de Beauvoir, an ex-dandy and man of letters, who talked incessantly during the whole of dinner time, as I remember, though I can't for the life of me recall what he said. Well we went together to the play, and he took me where William would long to go, to the green-room. I have never been in a French green-room before, and was not much excited, but when he proposed to take me up to the *loge* of a beautiful actress with sparkling eyes and the prettiest little *retroussé* nosey-posey in the world, I said to the *régisseur* of the theatre 'lead on'! and we went through passages and up stairs to the *loge*, which is not a box, but O! gracious goodness, a dressing room!— —

She had just taken off her rouge, her complexion was only a thousand times more brilliant, perhaps, the *peignoir* of black satin which partially enveloped her perfect form, only served to heighten &c, which it could but partially do &c. Her lips are really as red as &c, and not covered with paint at all. Her voice is delicious, her eyes, O! they flashed &c upon me, and I felt my &c, beating so that I could hardly speak. I pitched in, if you will permit me the phrase, two or three compliments however, very large and heavy, of the good old English sort, and *O! mon dieu* she has asked me to go and see her. Shall I go, or shan't I? Shall I go this very day at 4 o'clock, or shall I not? Well, I won't tell you, I will put up my letter before 4, and keep this piece of intelligence for the next packet.

The funeral takes place to-morrow, and as I don't seem to do much work here, I shall be soon probably on the wing, but perhaps I will take a week's touring somewhere about France, Tours and Nantes perhaps or elsewhere, or anywhere, I don't know, but I hope before I go to hear once more from you. I am happy indeed to hear how well you are. What a shame it was to assault my dear lady with my blue devils. Who could help looking to the day of failing powers, but if I last a few years, no doubt I can get a shelter somewhere against that certain adversity, and so I ought not to show you my glum face or my dismal feelings. That's the worst of habit and confidence. You are so kind to me that I like to tell you all, and to think that in good or ill fortune I have your sympathy. Here's an opportunity for sentiment, here's just a little bit of the page left to say something neat and pretty. *Je les méprise les jolis mots, vous en ai-je jamais fait de ma vie? Je les laisse à Monsieur Bullar et ses pareils—j'en ferai pour Mademoiselle Page, pour la ravissante la sémillante la frétillante Adèle (c'est ainsi qu'elle se nomme) mais pour vous? Allons—partons—il est quatre heures— fermons la lettre—disons adieu, l'amie et moi—vous m'écrirez avant mon départ n'est ce pas? Allez bien, dormez bien, marchez bien, s'il vous plait, et gardy mwaw ung petty moreso de voter cure.* W. M. T.

PARIS, [1849]

As my mother wants a line from me, and it would cost me no more to write on two half sheets than one whole one, common economy suggests that I should write you a line to say that I am pretty well, and leading, as before, a dismal but dutiful life. I go and sit with the old Scotch widower every night, and with my aunt afterwards. This isn't very amusing, but the sense of virtue and self-denial tickles one, as it were, and I come home rather pleased to my bed of a night. I shall stay here for a few days more. My tour will be to Boulogne, probably, where I shan't find the Crowes, who are going away, but shall have Mrs. Procter; and next week will see me back in London probably, working away as in the old way.

Yesterday I went a little way into the country to see Miss R's husband, my old friend S. They have just got a little son, a beautiful child, and the happiness of this couple was pleasant, albeit somehow painful, to witness. She is a very nice, elegant accomplished young lady, adoring her Augustus, who is one of the best and kindest of old snobs. We walked across vines to the coach at half past seven o'clock, after an evening of two hours and a half, which was quite enough for me. She is a little thing, and put me in mind of my own wife somehow. Give Mrs. Fanshawe, with my respectful love, a good account of her cousin. I am bound to-day to another country place, but don't like the idea of it. Tomorrow I dine with Mr. T. B. Macaulay, who is staying in this hotel.

And what else has happened? I have been to see the actress, who received us in a yellow satin drawing room, and who told me that she had but one fault in the world, that she had *trop bon cœur*, and I am ashamed to say that I pitched in still stronger compliments than before, and I daresay that she thinks the enormous old Englishman is rapturously in love with her; but she will never see him again, that faithless giant. I am past the age when Fotheringays inflame, but I shall pop her and her boudoir into a book some day, and that will be the end of our transactions. A good character for a book accompanied us to the funeral, an expatriated parson, very pompous, and feeble-minded: who gets his living by black jobs entirely and attends all the funerals of our countrymen; he has had a pretty good season and is tolerably cheerful. I was struck by "Behold I show you a mystery" and the noble words subsequent, but my impression is, that St. Paul fully believed that the end of things and the triumph of his adored master, was to take place in his own time, or the time of those round about him. Surely St. John had the same feeling, and I suppose that this secret passed fondly among the initiated, and that they died hoping for its fulfilment. Is this heresy? Let his reverence tell me.

Madame, if you will be so diffident about your compositions there is no help for it. Your letter made me laugh very much, and therefore made me happy. When I saw that nice little Mrs. S. with her child yesterday, of course I thought about somebody else. The tones of a mother's voice speaking to an infant, play the deuce with me somehow; that charming nonsense and tenderness work upon me until I feel like a woman or a great big baby myself,—fiddledeedee. . . .

And here the paper is full and we come to the final G. B. Y.

I am always,
W. M. T.

[*Paris, September* 14, 1849.]

MY DEAR LADY:

This letter doesn't count, though it's most *probbly* the last of the series. Yesterday I couldn't write for I went to Chambourcy early in the morning to see those two poor Miss Powers, and the poor old faded and unhappy D'Orsay, and I did not return home till exactly 1 minute before post time, perhaps 2 late for the letter which I flung into the post last night. And so this is the last of the letters and I am coming back immediately. The last anything is unpleasant. . . .

I was to have gone to-morrow for certain to Boulogne, at least, but a party to Fontainebleau was proposed—by whom do you think?—by the President himself, I am going to dine with him to-day, think of that! I believe I write this for the purpose solely of telling you this,—the truth is I have made acquaintance here with Lord Douglas, who is very good natured, and I suppose has been instigating the President to these hospitalities. I am afraid I disgusted Macaulay yesterday at dinner, at Sir George Napier's. We were told that an American lady was coming in the evening, whose great desire in life, was to meet the author of *Vanity Fair*, and the author of the *Lays of A. Rome*, so I proposed to Macaulay to enact me, and to let me take his character. But he said solemnly, that he did not approve of practical jokes, and so this sport did not come to pass. Well, I shall see you at any rate, some day before the 23d., and I hope you will be happy at Southampton enjoying the end of the autumn, and I shall be glad to smoke a pipe with old Mr. Williams too, for I don't care for new acquaintances, whatever some people say, and have only your house now where I am completely at home. I have been idle here, but I have done plenty of dutifulness, haven't I? I must go dress myself and tell old Dr. Halliday that I am going to dine with the President, that will please him more than even my conversation this evening, and the event will be written over to all the family before long, be sure of that. Don't you think Mr. Parr will like to know it, and that it will put me well with him? Perhaps I shall find the grand cross of the Legion of Honor under my plate, I will put it on and come to you in it in that case.

I was going to have the impudence to give you a daguerreotype of myself which has been done here, very like and droll it looks, but it seemed to me too impertinent, and I gave it to somebody else. I've bought William four glasses to drink beer out of, since I never can get one of the silver ones when I come; don't let him be alarmed, these only cost a shilling apiece, and two such loves of *eau de Cologne* bottles for Mrs. Procter, and for my dear Mrs. Brookfield I have bought a diamond necklace and earrings,—I have bought you nothing but the handkerchiefs but I hope you will let me give you those, won't you?

I was very sorry for Turpin, I do feel an interest in her, and I think she is very pretty, all this I solemnly vow and protest. My paper is out, here's the last corner of the last letter. I wonder *who* will ask me to dine on Monday next.

October 31st. [1849]

MY DEAR MONSIEUR ET MADAME:

Harry says that you won't eat your dinner well if I don't write and tell you that I am thriving, and though I don't consider this a letter at all but simply a message, I have to state that I am doing exceedingly well, that I ate a mutton chop just now in Harry's presence with great gusto, that I slept

12 hours last night and in fact advance by steps which grow every day more firm toward convalescence. If you will both come down here I will give you beautiful rooms and the best of mutton.—I shall stop till Monday certainly, after which I may probably go to the club.

G. B. Y. Both on you.
W. M. T.

[Probably from Brighton after serious illness.]

[Dec: 1849]

MY DEAR LADY:

The weather is so fine and cheerful that I have made my mind up to go down to Brighton tomorrow, or somewhere where I can be alone, and think about my friend Mr. Pendennis, whom I have been forced to neglect. I have been working now until seven o'clock and am dead beat, having done a poor dawdling day's work, writing too much, hipped, hacked and blue-devilled. I passed Portman Street after an hour's ride in the Park but hadn't time to come in, the infernal taskmaster hanging over me; so I gave my bridle reins a shake and plunged into doggerel. Good bye God bless you, come soon back both of you. Write to me won't you? I wish a Merry Christmas for you and am

always yours,
W. M. T.

My dear Madam

It was as I feared on Friday, the little Printer's devil barred my door and I could not come out as I should have liked very much to meet Colonel Croustade — Colonel — I mean, — whom I have already had the pleasure of meeting at your house with an exterior w'h the world would call crusty

[A note and sketch sent by Thackeray to Mrs. Elliot, in the possession of Miss Kate Perry.]

" This note and sketch, and those on pp. 72 and 142, were written and drawn for my friends Mrs. Elliot and her sister Miss Perry, who has kindly sent them to me, to add to my own letters, as they belong to the same period of Mr. Thackeray's life."—
J. O. B.

I know of no person who is inwardly so richly endowed as M. de Cronstadt.

Meeting Kinglake yesterday (or was it the day before?) in the Park, we agreed that I should ask you if you would be so good as to receive me at dinner, or T if your table is full, on Friday: it is the first day I have when I am disengaged.

As I am in the act of writing this very last line the post man brings me your note.. but on Wednesday I am going to a party of authors: and must not be faithless to my friends & brethren. Is there still hope for our dear Miss Berry?.

Always most faithfully yours
W M Thackeray

Fragment.

[*Christmas*, 1849]

I stop in the middle of Costigan with a remark applied to readers of Thomas à Kempis and others, which is, I think, that cushion-thumpers and High and Low Church extatics, have often carried what they call their love for Δ to what seems impertinence to me. How good my —— has been to me in sending me a back ache,—how good in taking it away, how blessed the spiritual gift which enabled me to receive the sermon this morning,—how trying my dryness at this afternoon's discourse, &c. I say it is awful and blasphemous to be calling upon Heaven to interfere about the thousand trivialities of a man's life, that —— has ordered me something indigestible for dinner, (which may account for my dryness in the afternoon's discourse); to say that it is Providence that sends a draught of air upon me which gives me a cold in the head, or superintends personally the action of the James' powder which makes me well. Bow down, Confess, Adore, Admire, and Reverence infinitely. Make your act of faith and trust. Acknowledge with constant awe the idea of the infinite Presence over all.—But what impudence it is in us, to talk about loving God enough, if I may so speak. Wretched little blindlings, what do we know about Him? Who says that we are to sacrifice the human affections as disrespectful to God? The liars, the wretched canting fakirs of Christianism, the convent and conventicle dervishes,—they are only less unreasonable now than the Eremites and holy women who whipped and starved themselves, never washed, and encouraged vermin for the glory of God. Washing is allowed now, and bodily filth and pain not always enjoined; but still they say, shut your ears and don't hear music, close your eyes and don't see nature and beauty, steel your hearts and be ashamed of your love for your neighbour; and timid fond souls scared by their curses, and bending before their unending arrogance and dulness, consent to be miserable, and bare their soft shoulders for the brutes' stripes, according to the nature of women. You dear Suttees, you get ready and glorify in being martyrized. Nature, truth, love, protest day after day in your tender hearts against the stupid remorseless tyranny which bullies you. Why you dear creature, what a history that is in the Thomas à Kempis book! The scheme of that book carried out would make the world the most wretched, useless, dreary, doting place of sojourn—there would be no manhood, no love, no tender ties of mother and child, no use of intellect, no trade or science, a set of selfish beings crawling about avoiding one another and howling a perpetual *miserere*. We know that deductions like this have been drawn from the teaching of J. C., but please God the world is preparing to throw them over, and I won't believe them though they are written in ever so many books, any more than that the sky is green or the grass red. Those brutes made the grass red many a time, fancying they were acting rightly, amongst others with the blood of the person who was born today. Good-bye my dear lady and my dear old William.

Fragment.

[1850]

I was too tired to talk to Madam when I sent away the packet of MS to-day. I'm not much better now, only using her as pastime at a club half an hour before dinner. That's the way we use women. Well, I was rather pleased with the manuscript I sent you to-day, it seems to me to be good comedy, my mother would have acted in just such a way if I had run away with a naughty woman, that is I hope she would, though perhaps she is prouder than I am myself. I read over the first part of *Pendennis* to-day, all the Emily Costigan part, and liked it, I am glad to say; but I am shocked to think that I had forgotten it, and read it almost as a new book. I remembered allusions which called back recollections of particular states of mind. The first part of that book was written after Clevedon in 1848. . . . . .

What a wholesome thing fierce mental occupation is! Better than dissipation to take thoughts out of one; only one can't always fix the mind down and other thoughts will bother it. Yesterday I sat for six hours and could do no work; I wasn't sentimentalizing but I couldn't get the pen to go, and at four, rode out into the country and saw, whom do you think? O! lâche, coward, sneak, and traitor, that pretty Mrs. M. I wrote you about. The night before in the same way, restless and wandering *aventurier* (admire my constant use of French terms), I went to Mrs. Prinsep's and saw Virginia, then to Miss Berrys' and talked to Lord Lansdowne who was very jolly and kind.

. . . .

Then to Lady Ashburton, where were Jocelyns just come back from Paris, my lady in the prettiest wreath.—We talked about the Gorham controversy, I think, and when the Jocelyns were gone about John Mill's noble Article in the *Westminster Review;* an article which you mustn't read, because it will shock your dear convictions, but wherein, as it seems to me, a great soul speaks great truths; it is time to begin speaking truth I think. Lady Ashburton says not. Our Lord spoke it and was killed for it, and Stephen, and Paul, who slew Stephen. We shuffle and compromise and have Gorham controversies and say, "let things go on smoothly," and Jock Campbell writes to the Mother-Superior, and Milman makes elegant after-dinner speeches at the Mansion House—humbugs all! I am becoming very stupid and rabid, dinner-time is come; such a good dinner, truth be hanged! Let us go to Portland Place.

[*July*, 1850]

MY DEAR LADY:

I have had a bad week and a most cruel time of it this month; my groans were heart-rending, my sufferings immense; I thought No. XIX would never be born alive;—It is, but stupid, ricketty, and of feeble intellect, I fear. Isn't that a pretty obstetrical metaphor? Well, I suppose I couldn't get on because I hadn't you to come and grumble to. You see habit does so much, and though there is Blanche Stanley to be sure, yet shall I tell you,—I will though perhaps you won't believe it—I haven't been there for a month. And what a singular thing it is about my dear friend Miss F.—that I never spoke to her but once in my life when I think the weather was our subject—and as for telling her that I had drawn Amelia from anybody of our acquaintance I should have as soon thought of—of what? I have been laboriously crossing all my t's, *see*, and thinking of a simile. But it's good fun about poor little B. Does any body suppose I should be such an idiot as to write verses to her? I never wrote her a line. I once drew one picture in her music book, a caricature of a spoony song, in which I laughed at her, as has been my practice—alas! . . .   The only person to whom I remember having said anything about Amelia was the late Mrs. Bancroft, as I told you, and that was by a surprise.

Yesterday after a hard day's labour went out to Richmond; dined with old Miss Berrys. Lord Brougham there, enormously good fun, boiling over with humour and mischief, the best and wickedest old fellow I've met, I think. And I was better in health than I've been for a fortnight past. O! how I should like to come on Sunday by the Excursion train, price 5/, and shake hands and come back again! I've been working Pen all the morning and reading back numbers in order to get up names &c., I'd forgotten. I lit upon a very stupid part I'm sorry to say; and yet how well written it is! What a shame the author don't write a complete good story. Will he die before doing so? or come back from America and do it?—

And now on account of the confounded post regulations—I shan't be able to hear a word of you till Tuesday. It's a sin and a shame to cut 2 days out of our week as the Pharisees do—and I'll never forgive Lord John Russell, never.—The young ladies are now getting ready to walk abroad with their dear Par.—It is but a hasty letter I send you dear lady, but my hand is weary with writing Pendennis—and my head boiling up with some nonsense that I must do after dinner for Punch. Isn't it strange that, in the midst of all the selfishness, that one of doing one's business, is the strongest of all. What funny songs I've written when fit to hang myself!

Thursday.

As I am not to come back till Saturday, and lest you should think that any illness had befallen me, dear lady, I send you a little note. This place is as handsome as man could desire; the park beautiful, the quizeen and drinks excellent, the landlord most polite and good natured, with a very winning simplicity of manner and bonhomie, and the small select party tolerably pleasant. Charles Villiers, a bitter Voltairian joker, who always surprises one into laughter; —Peacock—did you ever read Headlong Hall and Maid Marian?—a charming lyrical poet and Horatian satirist he was when a writer; now he is a whiteheaded jolly old worldling, and Secretary to the E. India House, full of information about India and everything else in the world. There are 4 or 5 more, 2 young lords,—one extremely pleasant, gentleman-like, and modest, who has seen battles in India and gives himself not the least airs;—and there are the young ladies, 2 pretty little girls, with whom I don't get on very well though, —nor indeed with anybody over well. There's something wanting, I can't tell you what; and I shall be glad to be on the homeward way again, but they wouldn't hear of my going on Friday, and it was only by a strong effort that I could get leave for Saturday.

This paper you see is better, I bought it regardless of expense—half a ream of it, at Bristol.

That Bristol terminus is a confounding place. I missed the train I was to go by, had very nearly gone to Exeter and was obliged to post twenty-five miles in the dark, from Chippenham, in order to get here too late for dinner. Whilst I am writing to you what am I thinking of? Something else to be sure, and have a doggrel ballad about a yellow " Post

Chay" running in my head which I ought to do for Mr. Punch.

We went to the little church yesterday, where in a great pew with a fire in it, I said the best prayers I could for them as I am fond of. I wish one of them would get well . . . I must give my young ones three or four weeks of Paris and may go a travelling myself during that time; for I think my dear old mother will be happier with the children and without their father, and will like best to have them all to herself. Mon dieu, is that the luncheon bell already? I was late at dinner yesterday, and late at breakfast this morning. It is eating and idling all day long, but not altogether profitless idling, I have seen winter woods, winter landscapes, a kennel of hounds, jolly sportsmen riding out a hunting, a queer little country church with a choir not in surplices but in smock-frocks, and many a sight pleasant to think on.—I must go to lunch and finish after, both with my dear lady and the yellow po'chay.

Will Mr. and Mrs. Brookfield come and dine with Mr. Thackeray on Saturday? He will arrive by the train which reaches London at 5.25, and it would be very, very pleasant if you could come—or one of you, man or woman. Meanwhile I close up my packet with a g. b. y. to my dear lady and a kiss to Miss Brookfield, and go out for a walk in the woods with a noble party that is waiting down-stairs. The days pass away in spite of us, and we are carried along the rapid stream of time, you see. And if days pass quick, why a month will, and then we shall be cosily back in London once more, and I shall see you at your own fire, or lying on your own sofa, very quiet and calm after all this trouble and turmoil. God bless you, dear lady and William, and your little maiden.

W. M. T.

26 February, 1850.

After hearing that Miss Brookfield was doing well in the arms of her Mamma, if you please, I rode in the Park on Tuesday, where there was such a crowd of carriages along the Serpentine, that I blushed to be on horseback there, and running the gauntlet of so many beauties. Out of a thousand carriages I didn't know one, which was odd, and strikes one as showing the enormity of London. Of course if there had been anybody in the carriages I should have known them, but there was nobody, positively nobody. (This sentence isn't as neatly turned as it might have been, and is by no means so playfully satirical as could be wished.) Riding over the Serpentine Bridge, six horsemen, with a lady in the middle, came galloping upon me, and sent me on to the foot pavement in a fright, when they all pulled up at a halt, and the lady in the middle cried out, How do you do Mr. &c. The lady in the middle was pretty Mrs. L.. She made me turn back with the six horsemen ; of course I took off my hat with a profound bow, and said that to follow in her train was my greatest desire—and we rode back, all through the carriages, making an immense clatter and sensation, which the lady in the middle, her name was Mrs. Liddle, enjoyed very much. She looked uncommonly handsome, she had gentlemen with moustachios on each side of her. I thought we looked like Brighton bucks or provincial swells, and felt by no means elated.

Then we passed out of Hyde Park into the Green Ditto, where the lady in the middle said she must have a canter, and off we set, the moustachios, the lady, and myself, skurrying the policemen off the road and making the walkers stare. I was glad when we got to St. James' Park gate, where I could take leave of that terrific black-eyed beauty, and ride away by myself. As I rode home by the Elliot's I longed to go in and tell them what had happened, and how it was your little girl's birth-day ; but I did not, but came home and drank her health instead, and wrote her a letter and slept sound.

Yesterday after writing for three hours or so, what did I go out for to see ? First the Miss Jingleby's, looking very fresh and pretty ; you see we have consolations ; then a poor fellow dying of consumption. He talked as they all do, with a jaunty, lively manner, as if he should recover ; his sister sat with us, looking very wistfully at him as he talked on about hunting, and how he had got his cold by falling with his horse in a brook, and how he should get better by going to St. Leonard's ; and I said of course he would, and his sister looked at him very hard. As I rode away through Brompton, I met two ladies not of my acquaintance, in a brougham, who nevertheless ogled and beckoned me in a very winning manner, which made me laugh most wonderful. O! you poor little painted Jezebels, thinks I, do you think you can catch such a grey-headed old fogey as me? poor little things. Behind them came dear, honest, kind Castlereagh, galloping along ; he pulled up and shook hands ; that good fellow was going on an errand of charity and kindness, consumption hospital, woman he knows to get in, and so forth. There's a deal of good in the wicked world, isn't there ? I am sure it is partly because he is a lord that I like that man ; but it is his lovingness, manliness, and simplicity which I like best. Then I went to Chesham Place, where I told them about things. You ought to be fond of those two women, they speak so tenderly of you. Kate Perry is very ill and can scarcely speak with a sore throat ; they gave me a pretty bread tray, which they have carved for me, with wheat-ears round the edge, and W. M. T. in the centre. O! yes, but before that I had ridden in the Park, and met dear old Elliotson, thundering along with the great horses, at ten miles an hour. The little 'oss trotted by the great 'osses quite easily though, and we shook hands at a capital pace, and talked in a friendly manner, and as I passed close by your door, why I just went in and saw William and Mrs. F. Then at eight o'clock, a grand dinner in Jewry. . . . . My! what a fine dinner, what plate and candelabra, what a deal of good things, and sweetmeats especially wonderful. The Christians were in a minority. Lady C. beautiful, serene, stupid old lady; she asked Isn't that the great Mr. Thackeray? O! my stars think of that! Lord M—— H—— celebrated as a gourmand; he kindly told me of a particular dish, which I was not to let pass, something *à la Pompadour*, very nice. Charles Villiers, Lady Hislop, pretty little Hattie Elliot, and Lady Somebody,—and then I went to Miss Berrys'—Kinglake, Phillips, Lady Stuart de Rothesay, Lady Waterford's mother, Colonel Damer. There's a day for you. Well, it was a very pleasant one, and perhaps this gossip about it, will amuse my dear lady.

[Written to Mrs. Fanshawe and Mrs. Brookfield.]

HÔTEL BRISTOL, PLACE VENDÔME.

Tuesday, March 5th. 1850

MY DEAR LADIES:

I am arrived just this minute safe and sound under the most beautiful blue sky, after a fair passage and a good night's rest at Boulogne, where I found, what do you think?—a letter from a dear friend of mine, dated September 13th, which somehow gave me as much pleasure as if it had been a fresh letter almost, and for which I am very much obliged to you. I travelled to Paris with a character for a book, Lord Howden, the ex-beau Caradoc or Cradock, a man for whom more women have gone distracted than you have any idea of. So delightful a middle-aged dandy! Well, he will make a page in some book some day. In the meantime I want to know why there is no letter to tell me that madame is getting on well. I should like to hear so much. It seems a shame to have come away yesterday without going to ask. It was the suddenest freak, done, packed and gone in half an hour, hadn't time even to breakfast. . . . And as I really wanted a little change and fresh air for my lungs, I think I did well to escape. . . . .

I send this by the Morning Chronicle's packet. Don't be paying letters to me, but write & write away, and never mind the expense, Mrs. Fanshawe.

W. M. T.

HÔTEL BRISTOL, PLACE VENDÔME.

[1850]

MADAME:

One is arrived, one is at his ancient lodging of the Hôtel Bristol, one has heard the familiar clarions sound at nine hours and a half under the Column, the place is whipped by the rain actually, and only rare umbrellas make themselves to see here and there; London is grey and brumous, but scarcely more sorrowful than this. For so love I these places, it is with the eyes that the sun makes itself on the first day at Paris; one has suffered, one has been disabused, but one is not blasé to this point that nothing more excites, nothing amuses. The first day of Paris amuses always. Isn't this a perfectly odious and affected style of writing?

Wouldn't you be disgusted to have a letter written all like that? Many people are scarcely less affected, though, in composing letters, and translate their thoughts into a pompous unfamiliar language, as necessary and proper for the circumstances of letter-writing. In the midst of this sentiment Jeames comes in, having been employed to buy pens in the neighbourhood, and having paid he said three francs for twenty.—I go out in a rage to the shop, thinking to confound the woman who had cheated him; I place him outside the shop and entering myself ask the price of a score of pens; one franc says the woman; I call in Jeames to confront him with the tradeswoman; she says, I sold monsieur a box of pens, he gave me a five-franc piece, I returned him two 2-franc pieces, and so it was; only Jeames never having before seen a two-franc piece, thought that she had given back two franc pieces; and so nobody is cheated, and I had my walk in the rain for nothing.

But as this had brought me close to the Palais Royal, where there is the exhibition of pictures, I went to see it, wondering whether I could turn an honest penny by criticising the same. But I find I have nothing to say about pictures. A pretty landscape or two pleased me; no statues did; some great big historical pictures bored me. This is a poor account of a Paris exhibition, isn't it? looking for half a minute at a work which had taken a man all his might and main for a year; on which he had employed all his talents, and set all his hopes and ambition; about which he had lain awake at night very probably, and pinched himself of a dinner that he might buy colours or pay models,—I say it seems very unkind to look at such a thing with a yawn and turn away indifferent; and it seemed to me as if the cold, marble statues looked after me reproachfully and said, " Come back, you sir! don't neglect me in this rude way. I am very beautiful, I am indeed. I have many hidden charms and qualities which you don't know yet, and which you would know and love if you would but examine a little." But I didn't come back, the world didn't care for the hidden charms of the statue, but passed on and yawned over the next article in the Catalogue. There is a moral to this fable, I think; and that is all I got out of the exhibition of the Palais Royal.

Then I went to beat up the old haunts, and look about for lodgings which are awfully scarce and dear in this quarter. Here they can only take me in for a day or two, and I am occupying at present two rooms in a gorgeous suite of apartments big enough and splendid enough for the Lord Chief Baron* and all his family. Oh! but first, I forgot, I went to breakfast with Bear Ellice, who told me Lady Sandwich had a grand ball, and promised to take me to a soirée at Monsieur Duchâtel's. I went there after dining at home. Splendid hotel in the Faubourg Saint Germain; magnificent drawing room; vulgar people, I thought; the walls were splendidly painted; "C'est du Louis Quinze ou du commencement de Louis XVI," the host said. *Blagueur!* the painting is about ten years old, and is of the highly ornamental Café school. It is a Louis Phillippist house, and everybody was in mourning—for the dear Queen of the Belgians, I suppose. The men as they arrived went up and made their bows to the lady of the house, who sat by the fire talking to other two ladies, and this bow over, the gentlemen talked, standing, to each other. It was uncommonly stupid. Then we went off to Lady Sandwich's ball. I had wrote a note to her ladyship in the morning, and received a Kyind invitation. Everybody was there, Thiers, Molé, and the French Sosoiatee, and lots of English; the Castlereaghs, very kind and hearty, my lady looking very pretty, and Cas—(mark the easy grace of Cas)—well, and clear-sighted; Lord Normanby and wife, exceeding gracious;—Lady Waldegrave;—all sorts

* The late Lord Chief Baron was the father of thirty-two children.

of world, and if I want the reign of pleasure, it is here, it is here. Gudin the painter asked me to dine today and meet Dumas, which will be amusing I hope.

And I forgot to say that Mr. Thomas Fraser says, that Mr. Inspector Brookfield is the most delightful fellow he ever met. I went to see my aunt besides all this, and the evening and the morning was the first day.

Sunday morning. I passed the morning yesterday writing the scene of a play, so witty and diabolical that I shall be curious to know if it is good; and went to the pictures again, and afterwards to Lady Castlereagh and other polite persons, finishing the afternoon dutifully at home, and with my aunt and cousins, whom you would like. At dinner at Gudin's there was a great stupid company, and I sat between one of the stupidest and handsomest women I ever saw in my life, and a lady to whom I made three observations which she answered with Oui, Monsieur, and non, monsieur, and then commenced a conversation over my back with my handsome neighbour. If this is French manners, says I, Civility be hanged, and so I ate my dinner; and did not say one word more to that woman.

But there were some pleasant people in spite of her: a painter (portrait) with a leonine mane, Mr. Gigoux, that I took a liking to; an old general, jolly and gentlemanlike; a humorous Prince, agreeable and easy: and a wonderful old buck, who was my pleasure. The party disported themselves until pretty late, and we went up into a tower fitted up in the Arabian fashion and there smoked, which did not diminish the pleasure of the evening. Mrs. L. the engineer's wife, brought me home in her brougham, the great engineer sitting bodkin and his wife scolding me amiably, about Laura and Pendennis. A handsome woman this Mrs L. must have been when her engineer married her, but not quite up to her present aggrandized fortune. . . . .

My old folks were happy in their quarter, and good old
G. P. bears the bore of the children constantly in his room,
with great good humour. But ah, somehow it is a dismal
end to a career. A famous beauty and a soldier who has
been in twenty battles and led a half dozen of storming parties! Here comes Jeames to say that the letters must this
instant go; and so God bless you and your husband and little maiden, and write soon, my dear kind lady, to
W. M. T.

[*Paris*, 1850]

I send this scrap by a newspaper correspondent, just to
say I am very well and so awfully hard at business I have no
time for more.

Wednesday.

MADAM AND DEAR LADY:

If I have no better news to send you than this, pray don't
mind, but keep the enclosures safe for me against I come
back, which won't be many days now, please God. I had
thought of setting off tomorrow, but as I have got into working trim, I think I had best stop here and do a great bit of
my number, before I unsettle myself by another journey. I
have been to no gaieties, for I have been laid up with a violent
cold and cough, which kept me in my rooms, too stupid even
to write. But these ills have cleared away pretty well now,
and I am bent upon going out to dinner *au cabaret*, and to
some fun afterwards, I don't know where, nor scarce what I
write, I am so tired. I wonder what will happen with Pendennis and Fanny Bolton; writing it and sending it to you,
somehow it seems as if it were true. I shall know more

about them tomorrow; but mind, mind and keep the manuscript; you see it is five pages, fifteen pounds, by the immortal Gods!

I am asked to a marriage tomorrow, a young Foker, of twenty-two, with a lady here, a widow, and once a runaway.

The pen drops out of my hand, it's so tired, but as the ambassador's bag goes for nothing, I like to say how do you do, and remember me to Miss Brookfield, and shake hands with William. God bless you all.

This note which was to have gone away yesterday, was too late for the bag, and I was at work too late today to write a word for anything but *Pendennis:* I hope I shall bring a great part of it home with me at the end of the week, in the meantime don't put you to the trouble of the manuscript, which you see I was only sending because I had no news and no other signs of life to give. I have been out to the play tonight, and laughed very pleasantly at nonsense until now, when I am come home very tired and sleepy, and write just one word to say good-night. . . . .

They say there is to be another revolution here very soon, but I shall be across the water before that event, and my old folks will be here instead. You must please to tell Mrs. Fanshawe that I am over head and ears in work, and that I beg you to kiss the tips of her gloves for me. There is another letter for you begun somewhere, about the premises, but it was written in so gloomy and egotistical a strain, that it was best burnt. I burnt another yesterday, written to Lady Ashburton, because it was too pert, and like Major Pendennis, talking only about lords and great people, in an easy off hand way. I think I only write naturally to one person now, and make points and compose sentences to others. That is why you must be patient please, and let me go on twaddling and boring you.

Dieppe
Hôtel [illegible]

For one there is some good in being in France dear lady, for I can write now a line on a Saturday night & know that it will travel through Sunday and reach you some time the next day. As yet the journey hasn't done me any good — on the contrary stirred up my innards much and made me ill — I was in bed the greater part of yesterday & to day and when I went to look at the town and sea we are very [fully?] only saw [lines?] with such bilious eyes as a man deserves who dines out every day of his life. Why didn't I accept your invitation on Wednesday instead of Wednesday? — it seems to me about 2 years since Wednesday — I thought I'd been to see you in the day. [illegible]! I'm always made [kindly?] welcome that I'd no business to come, and so instead went to the Rugge Famish, where without [recording?] I had exactly 4 times as much wine as was good for me and woke sick and ill and have been ill & sick ever since — now better. [illegible] the [illegible] — for I took a delightful drive into the country, & saw a beautiful old church and a charming [landscape?] and an [answered?] castle wh interested me only a very little (You may pass over the rest of this sentence and page if you please for I warn you that my intention is to menager you a surprise on the other side of the page and all this is my filling in as I have to do with my blocks in Pocadonnais Sometimes) Well I hired a gig and [went?] horse to drive me & who do you think was my driver?

("I've drawn it shockingly she thought I took the gold pen – but there was my Coachwoman a very lovely buxom girl whose name was Angelina Hewison and who told me she was heiress of fifteen horses and six carriages w: her Papa left.. As we were driving to Étretat we met one of the carriages and Angelina cried out Voici Papa – and I thought Papa looked a little queer at seeing his daughter drive a gentleman of forty. But she amused me with her artless prattle., and Papa did not know that I was suffering. from something not at all unlike Cholera

We made some of my greenness to Angelina ghastly to look at. However the drive did me good & the bracing air and scene, and Angelina if you like. There came to see me a lady before Angelina's arrival you must know. I found an elderly female waiting in the Hotel passage whom I instantly knew to be the wife of the Swedish clergyman of the place — an honest brawny and walrus divine whom I recognized at once (without having ever seen before) and whose acquaintance I made on the packet. I shall go to his church tomorrow, and if he is free to dine out of a Sunday, will fill his old skin with strong drink. The continental parson is a sort you don't know, uh, mum! he's very different to the white chokers of St James or Saintes les garets or Saint Montgomeryji! What a deal that woman has had to suffer. What insults from butchers and lodging house keepers whom his Rev even couldn't pay. What hate have gone forward for him — what struggles to be respectable. She has kept up since the day twenty years ago when that croaking old woman was a pretty fresh young lass! — Don't you see there is getting like a book? And am I not going to be able to write naturally even to you — my dear lady? Since I have been here I have read through 3 plays, those of Beaumarchais the Figaro cycle, and 2 novels one in 6 volumes very impudent and amusing by old Andre Dumas fils — and I have had letters from Mr James, a comportment as elegant as you could wish a his Reverence, and who forgot on my portmanteau just the things w! I told him to put there.

And now Mdme I dont like to ask you to write to me because I dont think I shall stop here very long — may come back by next Mondays packet but that would perhaps hurt the feelings of my old folks at Paris who might like to see me — And will you make me a birthday present please, and it shall be a dinner on the 18 Ik see you off with your wife, and there-fore away at Tenderness.

Coming here wont do. very moderate houses let at 50£ for the season. Then to go & come with my family is 20£ more. — Whereas he may go to Boulogne & back for 6£ and get rooms for 25£. And so god bless you, dear friend — and God bless all yours prays your affectionate brother Makepeace.

There was a little girl of 10 in the Railroad going to Eastbourne who was so beautiful that I had nearly gone after her, for I wanted very little to decide me one way or other, and only came hither because I saw by Bradshaw in the morning that the boat started on that day. But I think and hope I shall be better for the little change. There's a play here tomorrow night Sunday, will you come?

[*Paris*, 1850.]

MY DEAR LADY:

Do you see how mad everybody is in the world? or is it not my own insanity? Yesterday when it became time to shut up my letter, I was going to tell you about my elders, who have got hold of a mad old Indian woman, who calls herself Aline Gultave d'origine Mogole, who is stark staring mad, and sees visions, works miracles, *que sais-je?* The old fool is mad of sheer vanity, and yet fool as she is, my people actually believe in her, and I believe the old gentleman goes to her every day. To-day I went to see D'Orsay, who has made a bust of Lamartine, who, too, is mad with vanity. He has written some verses on his bust, and asks, Who is this? Is it a warrior? Is it a hero? Is it a priest? Is it a sage? Is it a tribune of the people? Is it an Adonis? meaning that he is all these things,—verses so fatuous and crazy I never saw. Well, D'Orsay says they are the finest verses that ever were written, and imparts to me a translation which Miss Power has made of them; and D'Orsay believes in his mad rubbish of a statue, which he didn't make; believes in it in the mad way that madmen do,—that it is divine, and that he made it; only as you look in his eyes, you see that he doesn't quite believe, and when pressed hesitates, and turns away with a howl of rage. D'Orsay has fitted himself up a charming *atelier* with arms and trophies, pictures and looking-glasses, the tomb of Blessington, the sword and star of Napoleon, and a crucifix over his bed; and here he dwells without any doubts or remorses, admiring himself in the most horrible pictures which he has painted, and the statues which he gets done for him. I had been at work till two, all day before going to see him; and thence went to Lady Normanby, who was very pleasant and talkative; and then tramping upon a half dozen of visits of duty. I had refused proffered banquets in order to dine at home, but when I got home at the dinner hour, everybody was away, the *bonne* was ill and obliged to go to the country, and parents and children were away to dine with a Mrs. . . . a good woman who writes books, keeps a select boarding-house for young ladies who wish to see Parisian society, and whom I like, but cannot bear, because she has the organ of admiration too strongly. Papa was king, mamma was queen, in this company, I a sort of foreign emperor with the princesses my daughters. By Jove, it was intolerably painful; and I must go to her soirée to-morrow night too, and drag about in this confounded little Pedlington. Yesterday night,—I am afraid it was the first day of the week,—I dined with Morton, and met no less than four tables of English I knew, and went to the play. There was a little girl acting, who made one's heart ache; —the joke of the piece is, the child, who looks about three, is taken by the servants to a casino, is carried off for an hour by some dragoons, and comes back, having learned to smoke, to dance slang dances, and sing slang songs. Poor little rogue, she sung one of her songs, from an actor's arms; a wicked song, in a sweet little innocent voice. She will be bought and sold within three years from this time, and won't be playing at wickedness any more. I shall shut up my desk and say God bless all the little girls that you and I love, and their parents. God bless you, dear lady.

I have got a very amusing book, the *Tatler* newspaper of 1709; and that shall be my soporific I hope. I have been advancing in Blue Beard, but must give it up, it is too dreadfully cynical and wicked. It is in blank verse and all a diabolical sneer. Depend upon it, Helps is right.

Wednesday. If I didn't write yesterday it was because I was wickedly employed. I was gambling until two o'clock this morning, playing a game called *lansquenet* which is very good gambling; and I left off, as I had begun, very thankful not to carry away any body's money or leave behind any of my own: but it was curious to watch the tempers of the various players, the meanness of one, the flurry and excitement of another, the difference of the same man winning and losing; all which I got, besides a good dinner and a headache this morning. Annie and Minnie and my mother, came to see me yesterday. I don't think they will be so very eager for Paris after three weeks here; the simple habits of our old people will hardly suit the little women. Even in my absence in America, I don't quite like leaving them altogether here; I wonder if an amiable family, as is very kind to me, will give them hospitality for a month? I was writing Blue Beard all day; very sardonic and amusing to do, but I doubt whether it will be pleasant to read or hear, or even whether it is right to go on with this wicked vein; and also, I must tell you that a story is biling up in my interior, in which there shall appear some very good, lofty and generous people; perhaps a story without any villains in it would be good, wouldn't it?

Thursday.—Thanks for your letter madame. If I tell you my plans and my small gossip, I don't bore you do I? You listen to them so kindly at home, that I've got the habit, you see. Why don't you write a little handwriting, and send me yours? This place begins to be as bad as London in the season; there are dinners and routs for every day and night. Last night I went to dine at home, with *bouilli boeuf* and *ordinaire*, and bad ordinaire too; but the dinner was just as good as a better one, and afterwards I went with my mother to a *soirée*, where I had to face fifty people of whom I didn't know one; and being there, was introduced to other *soirée* givers, be hanged to them. And there I left my ma, and went off to Madame Gudin's the painter's wife, where really there was a beautiful ball; and all the world, all the English world that is; and to-night it is the President's ball, if you please, and tomorrow, and the next day, and the next, more gaieties. It was queer to see poor old Castlereagh in a dark room, keeping aloof from the dancing and the gaiety, and having his thoughts fixed on kingdom come, and Bennett confessor and martyr; while Lady Castlereagh, who led him into his devotional state, was enjoying the music and the gay company, as cheerfully as the most mundane person present. The French people all talk to me about *Ponche*, when I am introduced to them, which wounds my vanity, which is wholesome very likely. Among the notabilities was Vicomte D'Arlincourt, a mad old romance writer, on whom I amused myself by pouring the most tremendous compliments I could invent. He said, *j'ai vu l'Écosse; mais Valter Scott n'y était plus, hélas!* I said, *vous y étiez, Vicomte, c'etait bien assez d'un*—on which the old boy said I possessed French admirably, and knew to speak the prettiest things in the prettiest manner. I wish you could see him, I wish you could see the world here. I wish you and Mr. were coming to the play with me tonight, to a regular melodrama, far away on the Boulevard, and a quiet little snug dinner *au Banquet d'Anacréon*. The *Banquet d'Anacréon* is a dingy little restaurant on the boulevard where all the plays are acted, and they tell great things of a piece called *Paillasse* in which Le Maitre performs; *nous verrons*, Madame, *nous verrons*. But with all this racket and gaiety, do you understand that a gentleman feels very lonely? I swear I had sooner have a pipe and a gin and water soirée with somebody, than the best President's *orgeat*. I go to my cousins for half an hour almost every day; you'd like them better than poor Mary whom you won't be able to stand, at least if she talk to you about her bodily state as she talks to me. What else shall I say in this stupid letter? I've not

Lady of the House.

[Drawing by Thackeray in Mrs. Brookfield's possession (perhaps Lady Castlereagh?).]

seen any children as pretty as Magdalene, that's all. I have told Annie to write to you and I am glad Mrs. Fan is going to stay ; and I hear that several papers have reproduced the thunder and small beer articles ;* and I thank you for your letter ; and pray the best prayers I am worth for you, and your husband, and child, my dear lady.

W. M. T.

Tuesday [23rd April 1850]

Your Sunday's letter only came in this morning, I am sorry to see my dear lady writes *tristely*, but I would rather you would write sorrowfully if you feel so than sham gaiety or light-heartedness. What's the good of a brother to you, if you can't tell him things ? If I am dismal don't I give you the benefit of the dumps ? Ah ! I should like to be with you for an hour or two and see if you are changed and oldened, in this immense time that you have been away. But business and pleasure keep me here nailed. I have an awful week of festivities before me ; today Shakespeare's birthday at the Garrick Club, dinner and speech. Lunch, Madame Lionel Rothschild's ; ball, Lady Waldegrave's ; she gives the finest balls in London, and I have never seen one yet. Tomorrow, of five invitations to dinner, the first is Mr. Marshall, the Duke of Devonshire's evening party, Lady Emily Dundas' ditto. Thursday, Sir Anthony Rothschild. Friday, the domestic affections. Saturday, Sir Robert Peel. Sunday, Lord Lansdowne's. Isn't it curious to think—it was striking my great mind yesterday, as Annie was sorting the cards in the chimney-glass,—that there are people who would give their ears, or half their income to go to these fine places ? I was riding with an Old Bailey barrister, yesterday in the

---

* Thackeray's reply to a criticism in the *Times*.

Park, and his pretty wife (*on les aiment jolies, Madame*). He apologised for knowing people who lived in Brunswick Square, and thought to prove his gentility by calling it that *demned* place.

The good dinner on Friday was very pleasant and quiet with old acquaintances, the ladies, M. P.'s wives, took me aside and asked confidentially about the fashionable world in which it is supposed, I believe, that I live entirely now; and the wonder is that people don't hate me more than they do. I tried to explain that I was still a man, and that among the ladies of fashion, a lady could but be a lady, and no better nor no worser. Are there any better ladies than you and Pincushion? Annie has found out that quality in the two of you, with her generous instincts. I had a delightful morning with her on Sunday, when she read me the *Deserted Village*, and we talked about it. I couldn't have talked with her so, with anybody else, except perhaps you, in the room. Saturday! what did I do? I went to Punch and afterwards to a play, to see a piece of the *Lady of Lyons* performed, by a Mr. Anderson. Before that to the Water-Colour Society, which was choke-full of bishops and other big-wigs, and among them Sir Robert Peel elaborately gracious,—conversation with Lady Peel, about 2000 people looking on. Bows, grins, grimaces on both sides, followed by an invitation to dinner next Saturday. The next person I shook hands with after Sir Robert Peel, was—who do you think? Mrs. Rhodes of the Back Kitchen; I thought of you that very instant, and to think of you, dear lady, is to bless you.

. . . . .

After, in going home from the Berrys, where was a great assembly of polite persons, Lady Morley, whom you love, (we laughed and cracked away so that it would have made you angry) my dear Elliot, and Perry, Lord Lansdowne, Carlyle, ever so many more. Oh! stop, at the Water Colours on Saturday, Mr. Hallam asked me to dinner. He and Lord Mohun and Miss Julia went and admired a picture, O! such a spoony picture. Sunday I went to Hampstead with the infants, and dined at the Crowes'; I went to Higgins', a very pleasant little party; sorry his reverence could not come. And then, which is I believe Monday, I was alarmed at not getting my manuscript back; I drew wood blocks all day, rode in the Park for three hours without calling or visiting anywhere; came home to dinner, went to the Berrys's and am back again at twelve, to say G. B. Y.

[1850]

CAMBRIDGE.

MADAM:

I have only had one opportunity of saying how do you do to-day, on the envelope of a letter which you will have received from another, and even more intimate friend W. H. B. This is to inform you that I am so utterly and dreadfully miserable now he has just gone off at one o'clock to Norwich by the horrid mail, that I think I can't bear this place beyond tomorrow and must come back again.

We had a very pleasant breakfast at Dr. Henry Maine's and two well-bred young gents of the University, and broiled fowls and mushrooms, just as we remember them 200 years ago. . . .

I have had the meanness not to take a private room and write in consequence in the Coffee Apartment in a great state of disquiet. Young under-graduates are eating supper, chattering is going on incessantly. I wonder whether William is safe in the train, or will he come back in two minutes, too late for the conveyance. Yes, here he comes actually —no, it is only the waiter with a fresh supply of bitter beer for the young gents. Well, we brexfested with Mr. and Mrs. Maine, and I thought him a most kind, gentle, and lovable sort of man, so to speak, and liked her artlessness and simplicity. (Note that this is the same horrid ink of last night, which will blot.) and then we went to fetch walks over the ground, forgotten, and yet somehow well remembered. William says he is going to bring you down here, and you will like it and be very happy. . . .

Just now William, I was going to write *Villiam*, but I knew you wouldn't like it, says, "She is dining at Lady Monteagle's," so I said "Let us drink her health," and we did, in a mixture of ale and soda water, very good. There was a bagman asleep in the room, and we drank your health, and both of us said, "God bless her," I think this is the chief part of my transactions during the day. . . . I think I said we walked about in haunts once familiar. We went to the Union where we read the papers, then drove to the river where we saw the young fellows in the boats, then amidst the College groves and cetera, and peeped into various courts and halls, and were not unamused, but bitterly melancholious, though I must say William complimented me on my healthy appearance, and he for his part, looked uncommonly well.

I went then to see my relations, old Dr. Thackeray 75 years of age, perfectly healthy, handsome, stupid and happy, and he isn't a bit changed in twenty years, nor is his wife, strange to say. I told him he looked like my grandfather, his uncle, on which he said, "Your grandfather was by no means the handsomest of the Thackerays," and so I suppose he prides himself on his personal beauty. At four, we went to dine with Don Thompson in Hall, where the thing to me most striking was the — — if you please, the smell of the dinner, exactly like what I remember afore-time. Savoury odours

THE STATUETTE OF THACKERAY BY JOSEPH EDGAR BOEHM, R.A.

of youth borne across I don't know what streams and deserts, struggles, passions, poverties, hopes, hopeless loves and useless loves of twenty years! There is a sentiment suddenly worked out of a number of veal and mutton joints, which surprises me just as much as it astonishes you, but the best or worst of being used to the pen is, that one chatters with it as with the tongue to certain persons, and all things blurt out for good or for bad. You know how to take the good parts generously and to forget the bad, dear kind lady. . . .

Then we went to Jenny Lind's concert, for which a gentleman here gave us tickets, and at the end of the first act we agreed to come away. It struck me as atrociously stupid. I was thinking of something else the whole time she was jugulating away, and O! I was so glad to get to the end and have a cigar, and I wanted so to go away with Mr. Williams, for I feel entirely out of place in this town. This seems to me to be spoken all in a breath, and has been written without a full stop. Does it not strike you as entirely frantic and queer? Well, I wish I were back. . . .

I am going out to breakfast to see some of the gallant young blades of the University, and tonight, if I last until then, to the Union to hear a debate. What a queer thing it is. I think William is a little disappointed that I have not been made enough a lion of, whereas my timid nature trembles before such honours, and my vanity would be to go through life as a gentleman—as a Major Pendennis—you have hit it. I believe I never do think about my public character, and certainly didn't see the gyps, waiters and undergraduates whispering in hall, as your William did, or thought he did. He was quite happy in some dreary rooms in College, where I should have perished of *ennui*,—thus are we constituted. An old hook-nosed clergyman has just come into the Coffee-room, and is looking over my shoulder I think, and has put a stop to the sentence beginning "thus are we constituted &c.

Jenny Lind made £400 by her concert last night and has given £100 to the hospital. This seems rather pompous sort of piety, it would be better to charge people less than 31/6 for tickets, and omit the charity to the poor. But you see people are never satisfied (the hook-nosed clergyman has just addressed a remark) only I pitied my cousins the Miss Thackerays last night, who were longing to go and couldn't, because tickets for four or five of them in the second rows, would have cost as many guineas, and their father could not afford any such sum. . . . Present my best compliments to Mrs. Fanshawe. If you see Mrs. Elliot remember me to her most kindly, and now to breakfast.

Written to us, when we were at Cambridge. [1850.]

Wednesday, Midnight.

I have made an awful smash at the Literary Fund and have tumbled into 'Evins knows where;—It was a tremendous exhibition of imbecility. Good night. I hope you 2 are sound asleep. Why isn't there somebody that I could go and smoke a pipe to?

Bon Soir

But O! what a smash I have made!

I am talking quite loud out to myself at the Garrick sentences I intended to have uttered: but they wouldn't come in time.

After the fatal night of the Literary Fund disaster, when I came home to bed (breaking out into exclamations in the cab, and letting off madly, parts of the speech which wouldn't explode at the proper time) I found the house lighted up, and the poor old mother waiting to hear the result of the day.—So I told her that I was utterly beaten and had made a fool of myself, upon which with a sort of cry she said " No you didn't, old man,"—and it appears that she had been behind a pillar in the gallery all the time and heard the speeches ; and as for mine she thinks it was beautiful. So you see, if there's no pleasing everybody, yet some people are easily enough satisfied. The children came down in the morning and told me about my beautiful speech which Granny had heard. She got up early and told them the story about it, you may be sure ; *her* story, which is not the true one, but like what women's stories are.

I have a faint glimmering notion of Sir Charles Hedges having made his appearance somewhere in the middle of the speech, but of what was said I haven't the smallest idea. The discomfiture will make a good chapter for Pen. It is thus we make *flèche de tout bois ;* and I, I suppose every single circumstance which occurs to pain or please me henceforth, will go into print somehow or the other, so take care, if you please, to be very well behaved and kind to me or else you may come in for a savage chapter in the very next number.

As soon as I rallied from the abominable headache which the Free Masons tavern always gives, I went out to see ladies who are quite like sisters to me, they are so kind, lively and cheerful. Old Lady Morley was there and we had a jolly lunch, and afterwards one of these ladies told me by whom she sat at Lansdowne House, and what they talked about and how pleased, she, my friend was. She is a kind generous soul and I love her sincerely.

After the luncheon (for this is wrote on Saturday, for all yesterday I was so busy from nine till five, when my horse was brought and I took a ride and it was too late for the post) I went to see ———, that friend of my youth whom I used to think 20 years ago the most fascinating, accomplished, witty and delightful of men. I found an old man in a room smelling of brandy and water at 5 o'clock at ———, quite the same man that I remember, only grown coarser and stale somehow, like a piece of goods that has been hanging up in a shop window. He has had 15 years of a vulgar wife, much solitude, very much brandy and water I should think, and a depressing profession; for what can be more depressing than a long course of hypocrisy to a man of no small sense of humour? It was a painful meeting. We tried to talk unreservedly, and as I looked at his face I remembered the fellow I was so fond of.—He asked me if I still consorted with any Cambridge men; and so I mentioned Kinglake and one Brookfield of whom I saw a good deal. He was surprised at this, as he heard Brookfield was so violent a Puseyite as to be just on the point of going to Rome. He can't walk, having paralysis in his legs, but he preaches every Sunday, he says, being hoisted into his pulpit before service and waiting there whilst his curate reads down below.

I think he has very likely repented: he spoke of his preaching seriously and without affectation: perhaps he has got to be sincere at last after a long dark lonely life. He showed me his daughter of 15, a pretty girl with a shrewish face and bad manners. The wife did not show. He must have been glad too when I went away and I dare say is more scornful about me than I about him. I used to worship him for about 6 months; and now he points a moral and adorns a tale such as it is in Pendennis. He lives in the Duke of

—— park at —— and wanted me to come down and see him, and go to the Abbey he said, where the Duke would be so glad to have me.—But I declined this treat—O fie for shame! How proud we get! Poor old Harry ——! and this battered vulgar man was my idol of youth! My dear old Fitzgerald is always right about men, and said from the first that this was a bad one and a sham. You see, some folks have a knack of setting up for themselves idols to worship.

Don't be flying off in one of your fits of passion, I don't mean you.

Then I went to dine at ——'s, where were his wife and sister. I don't thing so much of the wife, though she is pretty and clever—but Becky-fied somehow, and too much of a *petite maitresse*. I suppose a deal of flattery has been poured into her ears, and numberless men have dangled round that pretty light little creature. The sister with her bright eyes was very nice though, and I passed an evening in great delectation till midnight drawing nonsense pictures for these ladies, who have both plenty of relish for nonsense. Yesterday, after working all day, and then going to the London Library to audit accounts—doesn't that sound grand?—and taking a ride, I came home to dinner, fell asleep as usual afterwards, slept for 12 hours, and am now going to attack Monsieur Pendennis. Here is the journal. Now Ma'm have you been amused? Is King's very fine? is Trinity better? did you have a nice T at Mrs. Maine's? When are you coming back? Lord and Lady Castlereagh came here yesterday, and I want you to come back, so that I may give them an entertainment; —for I told my lady that I wanted to show her that other lady mentioned in the Punch article as mending her husband's chest of drawers—but I said waistcoat.—Sir Bulwer Lytton called yesterday.

To-night I am going to the bar dinner, and shall probably make another speech.—I don't mind about failing there, so I shall do pretty well. I rode by Portman Street on Thursday. Please to write and let me know whether you'll dine on the 28th or the 30th, or can you give me both those days to choose from. And so God bless both on you.

(Signed 3 hands clasped.)

Fragment of a letter

About 1850

I could not come yesterday evening to ring at the door; for I did not return until 8 o'clock from the visit to the emigrant ship at Gravesend, and then I had to work until 12, and polish off Pendennis. There are always four or five hours work when it is over, and four or five more would do it all the good in the world, and a second, or third reading.

That emigrant business was very solemn and affecting; it was with difficulty I could keep my spectacles dry—amongst the people taking leave, the families of grave-looking parents and unconscious children, and the bustle and incidents of departure. The cabins in one of the ships had only just been fitted up, and no sooner done than a child was that instant born in one of them, on the very edge of the old world as it were, which it leaves for quite a new country, home, empire. You shake hands with one or two of these people and pat the yellow heads of the children (there was a Newcastle woman with eight of them, who interested me a good deal) and say " God bless you, shake hands, you and I shall never meet again in this world, go and do your work across the four months of ocean, and God prosper it." The ship drops down the river, it gives us three great cheers as we come away in the steamer with heavy hearts rather. In three hours more Mr. W. M. T. is hard at work at Punch office;

Mr. Parson Quikette has got to his night school at St. George's in the East; that beautiful gracious princess of a Mrs. Herbert is dressing herself up in diamonds and rubies very likely, to go out into the world, or is she up stairs in the nursery, reading a good book over the child's cradle? Oh! enormous, various, changing, wonderful, solemn world? Admirable providence of God that creates such an infinitude of men, it makes one very grave, and full of love and awe. I was thinking about this yesterday morning before six, when I was writing the last paragraph of Pendennis in bed, and the sun walked into the room and supplied the last paragraph with an allusion about you, and which I think means a benediction upon William, and your child, and my dear lady. God keep you.

As I am waiting to see Mrs. Bullar, I find an old review with an advertisement in it, containing a great part of an article I wrote about Fielding, in 1840 in the *Times*. Perhaps Madame will like to see it, and Mr. Williams. My wife was just sickening at that moment; I wrote it at Margate, where I had taken her, and used to walk out three miles to a little bowling-green, and write there in an arbour—coming home and wondering what was the melancholy oppressing the poor little woman. The *Times* gave me five guineas for the article. I recollect I thought it rather shabby pay, and twelve days after it appeared in the paper, my poor little wife's malady showed itself.

How queer it is to be carried back all of a sudden to that time, and all that belonged to it, and read this article over; doesn't the apology for Fielding read like an apology for somebody else too? God help us, what a deal of cares, and pleasures, and struggles, and happiness I have had since that day in the little sunshiny arbour, where, with scarcely any money in my pocket, and two little children, (Minnie was a baby two months old) I was writing this notice about Fielding. Grief, Love, Fame, if you like.—I have had no little of all since then (I don't mean to take the fame for more than it's worth, or brag about it with any peculiar elation.)

My dear Madam: On calling on our mutual friend Mrs. Procter, yesterday, she was polite enough to offer me a seat in her box at Drury Lane theatre this evening, when Her *Majesty* honours the play-house with a visit for the benefit of Mr. Macready. Shakespeare is always amusing, and I am told the aspect of the beef-eaters at the royal box is very *imposing.* I mentioned to Mrs. Procter that I had myself witnessed many entertainments of this nature, and did not very much desire to be present, but intimated to her that I had a friend who I believed was most anxious to witness Mr. Macready's performance in the *august presence* of the Sovereign. I mentioned the name of your husband, and found that she had *already*, with her usual politeness, dispatched a card to that gentleman, whom I shall therefore have the happiness of meeting this evening. But perhaps you are aware, that a *chosen few* are admitted *behind the scenes* of the theatre, where, when the curtain rises, they appear *behind the performers*, and with loyal hearts join in the national anthem, at the very feet of their Queen. My reverend friend has an elegant voice, perhaps he would like to lift it up in a chorus, which though performed in the *temple of Thespis*, I cannot but consider to be in the nature of a *hymn.* I send therefore a ticket of which I beg his polite acceptance, and am dear Madam, with the utmost respect,

Your very faithful servant,
W. M. Thackeray.

P. S. I was a little late for the magnificent entertainment of my *titled friends* Sir William and Lady Molesworth, on Saturday, and indeed the first course had been removed, when I made my appearance. The banquet was sumptuous in the extreme, and the company of the most select order. I had the happiness of sitting next to Clarence Bulbul Esq., M.P., and opposite was the most noble, the Marquis of Steyne. Fancy my happiness in the company of persons so *distinguished*. A delightful concert followed the dinner, and the whole concluded with a sumptuous supper, nor did the party separate until a late hour.

Written about the time when we were at Park Cottage Southampton

[1850]

As the Sunday Post is open again, I write you a word of good-bye—and send you a little commission. Please to give Dr. Bullar's Infirmary 30/ for me and the children,—or put that sum into his money-box at Prospect Place. I tried my very hardest to compose my mind and ballad in the railway but it was no use. I start for Antwerp at 9 tomorrow morning; shall be there at 6 or so on Monday; and sleep probably at Cologne or Bonn; and if anybody chooses to write to me at Frankfort, Poste Restante, I should get the letter I daresay.—Shall I send you Lady Kicklebury's Tour? I will if it is at all funny or pleasant, but I doubt if it will do for letters well. Oh how glum and dingy the city looks, and smoky and dreary! Yesterday as I walking in the woods with Mrs. Procter looking at the columns of the fir trees, I thought of the pillars here, and said " This place is almost as lonely as the Reform Club in September." But the difference to the feeling mind is very great betwixt the two solitudes, and for one I envy the birds in the Hampshire boughs—what rubbish!

Fragment.

We have been to Shoolbred's to buy a gown for granny. We have been to Madame Victorine's to order new dresses for ourselves. We have been to call at Mrs. Elliot's, Mrs. Prinsep's, Lady Rothschild's, Mr. H. Hallam's, Mrs. James's, Mrs. Pollock's, Lady Pollock's, and the young women are gone home, and I am expecting Mr. William to dine here. I have ordered such a nice dinner; we are to go to the Sartoris' afterwards. Will you go there next Friday? I think I shall go somewhere on Sunday, Monday and Tuesday, I have no engagements for those three days, isn't it wonderful? But I'll be magnanimous and not bother my dear lady's friends.

I saw Harry Hallam, he and the faithful Maine were reading hard. Maine wanted me to fix to go to his house on Friday the 4th May, but I wouldn't. Harry was very pleasant, jovial, and gracious. He has been speaking well of me to the Elliots'. The artful dodger, he knew they would tell me again. What kind women they are! They say they had a very nice letter from you; I didn't have a nice letter from you; and as for your letter to my mamma, which I read, O! ma'am, how frightened you were when you wrote it, and what for were you in a fright? You have brains, imagination, wit; how conceited it is to be afraid, then.

I saw my lovely VIRGINIA to-day, she was as kind and merry as ever. The children seemed to stare to hear me laugh and talk, I never do at home. . . .

MR. INSPECTOR,

Mr. Kenyon having called upon me to fix a day when you may have the honour of meeting me at his house, I have proposed Christmas Eve, and am with compliments to the *geehrte Frau Schulinspektorin*

Yours
W. M. T.

WHITE LION, BRISTOL,
Monday 1850.

MY DEAR LADY:

With the gold pen there's no knowing how and what I write, the handwriting is quite different and it seems as if one was speaking with a different voice. Fancy a man stepping up to speak to you on stilts and trying to make a bow, or paying you compliments through a Punch's whistle;—not that I ever do pay you a compliment, you know, but I can't or I shan't be able for a line or two to approach you naturally, and must skate along over this shiny paper.

I went to Clevedon and saw the last rites performed for poor dear Harry.—* I went from here, and waited at Candy's till the time of the funeral, in such cold weather! Candy's shop was full of ceaseless customers all the time—there was a little boy buying candles and an old woman with the toothache —and at last the moment drew nigh and Tinling in a scarf and hat-band driving himself down from the Court, passed the shop, and I went down to the church. It looked very tranquil and well ordained, and I had half an hour there before the procession came in view. Those ceremonies over a corpse—

* H. F. Hallam died 24th Oct. 1850.

the immortal soul of a man being in the keeping of God, and beyond the reach of all undertakers,—always appear to me shocking rather than solemn,—and the horses and plumes give me pain.—The awful moment was when the dear old father—the coffin being lowered into the vault where so much of his affection and tenderest love lies buried, went down into the cave and gave the coffin a last kiss;—there was no standing that last most affecting touch of Nature. . . . Mr. Hallam who had been up-stairs came down after an hour or two; and I was so sorry that I had decided on coming back to Bristol, when he asked me whether I wasn't going to stay? Why didn't I? I had written and proposed myself to Dean Elliot in the morning personally, and I find he is out of town on returning here in the coldest night to the most discomfortable inn, writing paper, gold pen. . . . Duty, Duty is the word, and I hope and pray you will do it *cheerfully*.

Now it is to comfort and help the weak-hearted, and so may your comforter and helper raise you up when you fall. I wonder whether what I said to you yesterday was true? I know what I think about the famous chapter of St. Paul that we heard to-day,—one glory of the sun, and another of the moon, and one flesh of birds and one of fish and so forth,—premature definitions—yearnings and strivings of a great heart after the truth. Ah me—when shall we reach the truth? How can we with imperfect organs? but we can get nearer and nearer, or at least eliminate falsehood.

To-morrow then for Sir John Cam Hobhouse. Write to me there, dear sister, and tell me you are cheerful and that your baby is well, and that you love your affectionate old brother. When will you see the children? to-morrow I hope. And now I will go to bed and pray as best I can for you and yours and your nieces and your faithful old Makepeace.

G. B. Y.

MEMORIAL TABLETS TO ARTHUR AND HENRY HALLAM IN CLEVEDON CHURCH.

1851.

I have no news to give for these two days, but I have been busy and done nothing. Virtue doesn't agree with me well, and a very little domestic roseleaf rumpled puts me off my work for the day. Yesterday it was, I forget what; to-day it has been the same reason; and lo! Saturday cometh and nothing is done. . . . We have been to the Zoölogical Gardens this fine day and amused ourselves in finding likenesses to our friends in many of the animals. Thank *Evns!* both of the girls have plenty of fun and humour; your's ought to have, from both sides of the house,—and a deal of good besides, if she do but possess a mixture of William's disposition and yours. He will be immensely tender over the child when nobody's by, I am sure of that. No father knows for a few months what it is, but they learn afterwards. It strikes me I have made these statements before.

We had a dull dinner at Lady ——'s, a party of —— chiefly; and O! such a pretty one, blue eyes, gold hair, alabaster shoulders and such a splendid display of them. Venables was there, very shy and grand-looking—how kind that man has always been to me!—and a Mr. Simeon of the Isle of Wight, an Oxford man, who won my heart by praising certain parts of *Vanity Fair* which people won't like. Carlyle glowered in in the evening; and a man who said a good thing. Speaking of a stupid place at the sea-side, Sandwich I think, somebody said "Can't you have any fun there?" "O! yes," Corry said, "but you must take it with you." A nice speech I think, not only witty but indicating a gay cheerful heart. I intend to try after that; *we* intend to try after that; and by action and so forth get out of that morbid dissatisfied condition. Now I am going to dress to dine with Lord Holland; my servant comes in to tell me it is time. He is a capital man, an attentive, alert, silent, plate-cleaning, intelligent fellow; I hope we shall go on well together, and that I shall be able to afford him. . . .

Boz is capital this month, some very neat pretty natural writing indeed, better than somebody else's again. By Jove, he is a clever fellow, and somebody else must and shall do better. Quiet, pleasant dinner at Lord Holland's; leg of mutton and that sort of thing, home to bed at 10.30, and tomorrow to work really and truly. Let me hear, please, that you are going on well and I shall go on all the better.

April 29th, 1851.

MADAM AND DEAR LADY:

Will you have a little letter to-day, or a long letter to-morrow? for there's only half an hour to post time.—A little letter to-day?—I don't wonder at poets being selfish, such as Wordsworth and Alfred.—I have been for five days a poet, and have thought or remembered nothing else but myself and my rhymes and my measure. If somebody had come to me and said, "Mrs. Brookfield has just had her arm cut off," I should have gone on with, Queen of innumerable isles, tidumtidy, tidumtidy, and not stirred from the chair. The children and nobody haven't seen me except at night; and now though the work is just done, (I am just returned from taking it to the *Times* office) I hardly see the paper before me, so utterly beat, nervous, bilious and overcome I feel; so you see you chose a very bad day ma'am for a letter from yours very sincerely. If you were at Cadogan Place I would walk in, I dare say, say God bless you, and then ask leave to go to sleep. Now you must be thinking of coming back to Pimlico soon, for the lectures are to begin on the 15th. I tried the great room at Willis's yesterday, and recited part of the multiplication table to a waiter at the opposite end, so as to try the voice. He said he could hear perfectly, and I daresay he could, but the thoughts somehow swell and amplify with that high-pitched voice and elaborate distinctness. As I perceive how poets become selfish, I see how orators become humbugs and selfish in their way too, absorbed in that selfish pursuit and turning of periods. It is curious to take these dips into a life new to me as yet, and try it and see how I like it, isn't it? Ah me, idleness is best; that is, quiet and repose of mind and somebody to love and be fond of, and *nil admirari* in fine. The gentlemen of the G. tell me, and another auditor from the Macready dinner, that my style of oratory was conspicuous for consummate ease and impudence, I, all the while feeling in so terrible a panic that I scarcely knew at the time what I was uttering, and didn't know at all when I sat down.—This is all I have to tell you about self, and ten days which have passed away like a fever. Why, if we were to let the poetic cock turn, and run, there's no end of it I think. Would you like me now to become a great—fiddlededee? no more egotisms Mr. M. if you please.

I should have liked to see your master on Sunday, but how could I? and Lord! I had such a headache, and Dicky Doyle came, and we went to Soyer's Symposium and the Crystal Palace together, where the great calm leviathan steam engines and machines lying alongside like great line of battle ships, did wonderfully move me; and I think the English compartment do beat the rest entirely, and that let alone our engines, which be incomparable, our painters, artificers, makers of busts and statues, do deserve to compare with the best foreign. This I am sure will interest and please Miss Brookfield very much. God bless that dear little lady. I would give two-pence to hear her say, "more tea." Oh, by the way can I have that young woman of whom Rossiter spoke? Mary goes away at the end of the week and a cook is coming, and I want a maid, but have had no leisure to think of one until now, when my natural affairs and affections are beginning to return to my mind, and when I am my dear lady's friend and servant,

W. M. T.

May, 1851.

AMIE:

I write you a little word after that Exhibition from home. . . . .

The ode has had a great success. What do you mean by "an ode as she calls it?" *Vive dieu*, Madame, it is either an ode or nix (the German for nothing.) And as for the Exhibition, which don't interest me at all so much, it was a noble, awful, great love-inspiring, gooseflesh-bringing sight. I got a good place by good luck and saw the whole affair, of which no particular item is wonderful; but the general effect, the multitude, the riches, the peace, the splendour, the security, the sunshine, great to see,—much grander than a coronation. The vastest and sublimest popular festival that the world has ever witnessed before. What can one say about it but commonplace? There was a Chinese with a face like a pantomime-mask and shoes, who went up and kissed the Duke of Wellington, much to the old boy's surprise.

And the Queen looked not uninteresting; and Prince Albert grave, handsome, and princely; and the Prince of Wales and the Princess Royal are nice children,—very eager to talk and observe they seemed. And while the Archbishop was saying his prayer, beginning with *Pater Noster*, which sounded, in that wonderful throng, inexpressibly sweet and awful, three Romish Priests were staring about them, with opera glasses; which made me feel as angry as the Jews who stoned Stephen.

I think this is all I have to say. I am *very* tired and the day not over, for I have promised the children to take them to the play, in recompense for their disappointment in not getting to the Exhibition, which they had hopes of seeing through my friend Cole.   .   .   .   .   .

.   .   .   .

[1851.]

REFORM CLUB.

MY DEAR SIR OR MADAM:

Pax vobiscum; ora pro nobis. If you go to the lecture to-day, will you have the fly? It will be only ever so little out of the fly's way to come for you: and will you fetch me from this place please, and will you send an answer by coachman to say whether you will come or no?

I had a gentle ride in the Park, and was all but coming to 15, but I thought I wouldn't get off my oss at any place save that where I am going to work, namely this here, until lecture time. Doyle will be in waiting at 4½ o'clock to let the stray sheep into the fold.

I am, yours
MAKEPEACE,
Bishop of Mealy Potatoes.

My Dear Lady:

I have been at work until now, eight o'clock. The house is very pleasant, Mr. and Mrs. G. bent on being so, the dinners splendacious, and what do you think I did yesterday? Please to tell Spring Rice this with my best regards, tomorrow. I thought over the confounded Erminia matter in the railroad, and wrote instantly on arriving here, a letter of contrition and apology to Henry Taylor for having made, what I see now, was a flippant and offensive allusion to Mrs. Taylor. I am glad I have done it. I am glad that so many people whom I have been thinking bigoted and unfair and unjust towards me, have been right, and that I have been wrong, and my mind is an immense deal easier.

My dear ——: Will you, I mean Mr. Brookfield, like to come to Mrs. S's sworry to-night? There will be very pretty music, and yesterday when I met her, I said I wanted her very much to go and sing to a sick lady of my acquaintance and she said she would with the greatest pleasure in the world; and I think it would be right if Mr. Brookfield should call upon her, and I am disengaged on Wednesday next either for evening or dinner, and Mrs. Sartoris' number is 99 Eaton Place, and I am,

Your obedient servant

W. M. Thackeray.

My dear Vieux:

I have told the *mouche* to call for me at the Punch office at eight, and to come round by Portman Street first. If you like you can come and we can go to a little play, a little something, to Hampstead even if you were up to it. If you'd like best to sit at home, I'd like to smoke a pipe with you; if you'd like best to sit at home alone, I can go about my own business, but don't mind choosing which way of the three you prefer, and

     Believe me, *hallis* yours
           W. M. T.

My dear sick Lady:

I send you 1, 2, 3, 4, 5, 6, 7, MSS just to amuse you for ten minutes. Annie's I am sure will; isn't it good? the perilous passage, and the wanting to see me. The letters are to ladies who bother me about the Bath and Wash-house *fête;* and the verses, marked 2, were written in a moment of depression—I wonder whether you will like No. 2?

Virginia wasn't at dinner after all, yesterday. Wasn't that a judgment on somebody? She stopped to take care of a sick sister she has; but I made myself as happy as circumstances admitted, and drank your health in a glass of Mr. Prinsep's excellent claret; one can't drink mere port this weather.

When you have read all the little papers, please put them back, and send them by the printer's devil to their owner. It has just crossed my mind that you may think it very conceited, my sending you notes to read, addressed to grand ladies, as if I was proud of my cleverness in writing them, and of being in a state of correspondence with such grand persons. But I don't want to show off, only to try and give you ever so little amusement, and I don't choose to think about what other people choose to think about.

Yours, dear Mrs. Brookfield,
W. M. Thackeray.

My dear Madam:

I am always thinking of Mrs. C— W— H— with a feeling of regard, so intense and incomprehensible, that feeble words cannot give it utterance, and I know that only a strong struggle with my interior and a Principle which I may say is based on the eternal data of perennial reminiscences, can keep this fluttering heart tolerably easy and secure. But what, what, is Memory? Memory without Hope is but a negative idiosyncracy, and Hope without Memory, a plant that has no root. Life has many such, but still I feel that they are too few; death may remove or in some way modify their poignancy; the future alone can reconcile them with the irrevocable fiat of yesterday, and tomorrow I have little doubt will laugh them into melancholy scorn. Deem not that I speak lightly, or that beneath the mask of satire, any doubt, any darkness, any pleasure even, or foreboding, can mingle with the depth of my truthfulness. Passion is but a hypocrite and a monitor, however barefaced.

Action, febrile continuous action, should be the pole star of our desolate being. If this is not reality, I know not what is. Mrs. C. W. H. may not understand me, but you will.

(Sketch by Thackeray, belonging to Mrs Broomfield.)

Fragment.

. . . . And is W. Bullar going to work upon you with his " simple mysticism ? " I don't know about the Unseen World; the use of the seen World is the right thing I'm sure!—it is just as much God's world and Creation as the Kingdom of Heaven with all the angels. How will you make yourself most happy in it? how secure at least the greatest amount of happiness compatible with your condition? by despising to-day, and looking up cloudward? Pish. Let us turn God's to-day to its best use, as well as any other part of the time He gives us. When I am on a cloud a-singing, or a pot boiling—I will do my best, and if you are ill, you can have consolations; if you have disappointments, you can invent fresh sources of hope and pleasure. I'm glad you saw the Crowes, and that they gave you pleasure;—and that noble poetry of Alfred's gives you pleasure (I'm happy to say ma'am I've said the very same thing in prose that you like— the very same words almost). The bounties of the Father I believe to be countless and inexhaustible for most of us here in life; Love the greatest. Art (which is an exquisite and admiring sense of nature) the next.—By Jove! I'll admire, if I can, the wing of a Cock-sparrow as much as the pinion of an Archangel; and adore God the Father of the earth, first; waiting for the completion of my senses, and the fulfilment of His intentions towards me afterwards, when this scene closes over us. So when Bullar turns up his i to the ceiling, I'll look straight at your dear kind face and thank God for knowing that, my dear; and though my nose is a broken pitcher, yet, Lo and behold there's a Well gushing over with kindness in my heart where my dear lady may come and drink. God-bless you,—and William and little Magdalene.

Fragment.

I have had the politest offer made me to go to Scotland, to Edinburgh, where there is a meeting of the *savants*—just the thing for me, you know; thence to the Highlands with Edward Ellice; thence to Miss Prince's friend, the Duchess, who is the most jovial, venerable, pleasant, and I should think too, a little wicked, old lady. And I suppose I could be franked through the kingdom from one grandee to another; but it don't seem much pleasure or rest, does it? Best clothes every day, and supporting conversation over three courses at dinner; London over again. And a month of solitary idleness and wandering would be better than that, wouldn't it? On the other hand it is a thing to do and a sight to see, sure to be useful professionally, some day or other, and to come in in some story unborn as yet.

I did the doggerel verses which were running in my head when I last wrote you, and they are very lively. You'd say the author must have been in the height of good spirits;—no, you wouldn't, knowing his glum habit and dismal views of life generally.

We are going on a little holiday excursion down the river to Blackwall, to board the American Packet-ship, the Southampton, I told you of before; and shake hands with the jolly captain, and see him out of the dock. Then the young ladies are going to *Don Giovanni* in the evening, and I to dine with the Earl of Carlisle, but I want quiet. . . .

Do you remember my telling you of O'Gorman Mahon, bidding some ladies to beware of me for I could talk a bird off a tree? I was rather pleased at the expression, but O'Gorman last Saturday, took me away out of Lord Palmerston's arms, with whom I was talking, and said that some ladies had informed him, that when he made use of that expression, my countenance assumed a look of the most diabolical rage and passion, and that I abused him, O'Gorman in the most savage manner. In vain I remonstrated, he'll believe it to the end of his life.

1851.

> Good Friday.

Yesterday evening in the bitter blast of the breeze of March, a Cavalier, whose fingers were so numbed that he scarce could hold the rein of his good steed, might have been perceived at a door in Portman Street in converse with a footman in dark green livery, and whose buttons bore the cognizance of the Well-known house of Brookfield. Clouded with care and anxiety at first the horse-man's countenance (a stalwart and grey-haired man he was, by our lady, and his face bore the marks of wounds received doubtless in early encounters) presently assumed a more cheerful aspect when he heard from the curly-pated servitor whom he interrogated that his Lady's health was better. "Gramercy" he of the steed exclaimed "so that she mend I am happy! happier still when I may behold her! Carry my duty, Fellow, to my Mistress' attendant, and tell her that Sir Titmarsh hath been at her gate." It closed upon him. The horse-man turned his charger's head home-ward, and soon was lost to view in the now lonely park.

I've been to church already with the young ones—had a fine ride in the country yesterday—am going to work directly this note goes off—and am exceedingly well and jolly in health. I think this is all my news. . . . Mrs. Elliot has been very bad but is mending. I dined there last night. She was on the sofa, and I thought about her kind face coming in to me (along side of another kind-face) when I was ill. What numbers of good folks there are in the world! Fred. Elliot would do anything, I believe, to help me to a place. Old Miss Berry is very kind too, nothing can be kinder; but I will go back to my poetry for Punch, such as it is, and say good-bye to my dear lady and Miss Brookfield and Mr.

W. M. T.

[1851.]

MESDAMES :

You mustn't trust the honest *Scotsman*, who is such a frantic admirer that nothing less than a thousand people will content him. I had a hundred subscribers and two hundred other people for the first lecture. Isn't that handsome? It is such a good audience that I begin to reflect about going to America so soon. Why, if so much money is to be made in this empire, not go through with the business and get what is to be had? The Melgunds I saw at the sermon, and the Edinburgh big-wigs in plenty. The M's live over the way, I go to see them directly and thank them. And I like to tell you of my good luck, and am always yours,

W. M. T.

Mr. Jeames de la Pluche presents respectful Comps to Mrs. Elliot and I am very sorry that he cannot accept your genteel and polight invitation it he is engaged as you will be glad to hear to meet Miss Virginia Pattle; and afterwards to go to a friendly Swoary where praps a reverend gents lady by name of Br—kf-ld may consool me for his igstreme disapintment in not meeting neither Mrs E nor Miss P

PS. Respectful Comps to the young lady who sang like a Sirius

PS. Genteel regards to Miss K.E.P.

[From a letter to Mrs. Elliot, now in the possession of her sister, Miss Kate Perry.]

15 July, 1851.

The happy family has scarce had a moment's rest since we left the St. Katherine's wharf, and this is wrote on board the steamer—— in the Rhine, with ever so many fine views at my back,—Minnie on t'other side writing to her grandmother, and Annie reading her father's works in the Tauchnitz edition. It has not been a very brilliant journey hitherto, but the little ones are satisfied, that's the main point. The packet to Antwerp was awful, a storm, and a jib carried away, and a hundred women being sick on the cabin floor all night. The children very unwell, but behaving excellently; their pa, tranquil under a table and not in the least sick, for a wonder.

We passed the day, Friday, at Antwerp, when I hope his reverence came home to you better. And it was very pleasant going about with the children, walking and lionising. Yesterday, we got up at five and rushed to Cologne; today we rose at four, and rushed to Mayence. We shall sleep at Wiesbaden or at Frankfurt tonight, as the fancy siezes me; and shall get on to Heidelberg, then to Basle, then to Berne, & so on to Como, Milan, Venice, if it don't cost too much money. I suppose you are going to church at this time, and know the bells of Knightsbridge are tolling. If I don't go to church myself (but I do, here, this instant, opposite the young ones) I know who will say a God bless me. . . . . .

I bought *Kickleburys, Rebecca and Rowena*, and the *Rhine Story* and read them through with immense pleasure. Do you know I think all three Capital, and R. and R. not only made me laugh but the other thing. Here's pretty matter to send a lady from a tour! Well, I know you like to hear my praises and I am glad to send them to you. They are putting off a flat-bottomed boat from the shore—they are putting out the tables for dinner. I will lock up my paper and finish my letter at some future halting-place, and so good-bye dear lady.

Wiesbaden. The first minute to myself since we came away, and that in a ground floor closet, where it has been like sleeping in the street,—the whole house passing by it. It is the Hôtel de la Rose. Annie and Minnie are put away somewhere in the top of the house, and this minute at six in the morning, on the parade, they have begun music. The drive hither last night from the steamer was the most beautiful thing which has happened to us yet, and a view of the Rhine at Sunset, seen from a height, as lovely as Paradise. This was the first fine day we have had, and the splendour of the landscape-colours something marvellous to gaze upon. If Switzerland is better than this, we shall be in a delirium. It is affecting to see Annie's happiness. My dear noble creature, always magnanimous and gentle. I sat with the children and talked with them about their mother last night. . . . It is my pleasure to tell them how humble-minded their mother was, how humble minded you are, my dear lady. They bid me to the bath, I rise, I put on my scarlet gownd, I go.

Thursday morning. Again six o'clock. *Heidelberg.* After the bath and the breakfast we discovered that we were so uncomfortable at that most comfortable inn the Rose, without having the least prospect of bettering ourselves, that we determined on quitting Wiesbaden, though Mrs. Stewart Mackenzie had arranged a party for us, to see the Duke's garden,—an earthly paradise according to her account,—and though in the walk, a taking his waters, whom should I see, but T. Parr, Esquire, and I promised to go and see him and your sister. But *Dieu dispose*, and we came off to Frankfurt and took a carriage there for two hours and a half and inspected the city and then made for Heidelberg which we reached at 6½, too late for anything but dinner and a sleep afterwards, in the noisiest street I ever *slep* in; and there were other causes for want of rest, and so I got me up at five and soothed myself with the pleasant cigar of morn.

My dear lady, the country is very pretty, *zwischen* Frankfurt and Heidelberg, especially some fantastical little mountains, the Melibocus range, of queer shapes, starting out of the plain, capped with darkling pine forests and ruined castles, covered with many coloured crops and based by peaceful little towns with old towers and walls. And all these things as I behold, I wish that somebody's eyes could see them likewise; and R! I should like a few days rest, and to see nothing but a shady wood and a tolerably stupid book to doze over.

We had Kingsley and his parents from Antwerp; a fine honest go-ahead fellow, who charges a subject heartily, impetuously, with the greatest courage and simplicity; but with narrow eyes (his are extraordinarily brave, blue and honest), and with little knowledge of the world, I think. But he is superior to us worldlings in many ways, and I wish I had some of his honest pluck. And so my stupid paper is full, and I send my love to you and yours.

Thursday, 17th. [July, 1851.]

Yesterday was a golden day, the pleasantest of the journey as yet. The day before we got to Baden-Baden; and I had a notion of staying, say two or three days, having found an agreeable family acquaintance or two, Madame de Bonneval, sister of Miss Galway, with whom we went to the hippodrome, & M. Martchenko, that nice Russian who gave me cigars and flattered me last year; but the weather beginning to be bad, and the impure atmosphere of the pretty, witty gambling place not good for my young ones, we came away by the Basel railroad in the first-class, like princes. A most delightful journey through the delicious landscape of plain and mountains, which seemed to Switzify themselves as we came towards here; and the day's rest here has not been least pleasant, though, or perhaps because, it rained all the morning and I was glad to lie on the sofa and smoke my cigar in peace. On Tuesday at Baden it was pretty. Having been on duty for five days, I went out for a solitary walk, and was finding myself *tant soit peu* tired of my dear little companions; and met Madame de Bonneval, who proposed a little tea, and a little society &c.; and when I came back to the inn, there was Annie, with Minnie on her knees, and telling her a story with a sweet maternal kindness and patience, God bless her. This touched me very much and I didn't leave them again till bedtime, and didn't go to the *rouge-et-noir* and only for half an hour to Monsieur and Madame de Bonneval,—from whose society I determined to escape next day,—and we agreed it was the pleasantest day we had had; and Minnie laid out the table of the first class carriage (they are like little saloons and delightful to travel in) with all the contents of the travelling bag, books, o de Cologne, ink &c.; and we had good trout for supper at nine o'clock;

and today, at two, we walked out and wandered very pleasantly for two hours and a half about the town and round it; and we are very hungry; and we hope the dinner bell will ring soon—and tomorrow I am forty years old, and hope to find at Berne a letter from my dear lady. You see one's letters must be stupid, for they are written only when I am tired and just come off duty; but the sweet young ones' happiness is an immense pleasure to me, and these calm sweet landscapes bring me calm and delight too; the bright green pastures, and the soft flowing river (under my window now) and the purple pine-covered mountains, with the clouds flickering round them—O! Lord! how much better it is than riding in the Park and going to dinner at eight o'clock! I wonder whether a residence in this country would ennoble one's thoughts permanently, and get them away from mean quarrels, intrigues, pleasures? make me write good books—turn poet perhaps or orator—and get out of that business of London—in which there is one good thing? Ah, one good thing, and God bless her always and always. I see my dear lady and her little girl; *pax* be with them. Is it only a week that we are gone, it seems a year.

Berne. Saturday 19th. Faucon.—I must tell you that I asked at Heidelberg at the post only by way of a joke, and never so much as expecting a half-penny worth of letter from you; but here I went off to the post as sure as fate. Thinks I, it being my birthday yesterday there must be a little something waiting for me at the *poste restante*, but the deuce a bit of a little something. Well I hope you're quite well, and I'm sure you'd write if something hadn't prevented you, and at Milan or at Venice I hope for better fortune. We had the most delightful ride yesterday from Basel, going through a country which I suppose prepares one for the splendider scenery of the Alps; kind good-natured little mountains, not too awful to look at, but encouraging in appearance, and leading us gradually up to the enormities which we are to contemplate in a day or two. A steady rain fell all day, but this, as it only served to make other people uncomfortable, (especially the six Belgian fellow-travellers in the *Bei-wagen*, which leaked, and in which they must have had a desperate time) rather added to our own pleasure, snug in the *coupé*. We have secured it for tomorrow to Lucerne, and today for the first time since our journey there's a fine bright sun out, and the sight we have already had of this most picturesque of all towns, gives me a zest for that fine walk which we are going to fetch presently. I have made only one sketch in this note; best not make foolish sketches of buildings, but look about and see the beautiful pictures done for you by Nature beneficent. It is almost the first place I have seen in Europe where the women actually wear costumes—in Rome only the women who get up for the painters dress differently from other folks. Travelling as Paterfamilias, with a daughter in each hand, I don't like to speak to our country folks; but give myself airs, rather, and keep off from them. If I were alone I should make up to everybody. You don't see things so well *à trois* as you do alone; you are an English gentleman; you are shy of queer-looking or queer-speaking people; you are in the *coupé;* you are an earl;—confound your impudence, if you had £5000 a year and were Tomparr, Esq., you could not behave yourself more high and mightily. Ah! I recollect ten years back, a poor devil looking wistfully at the few napoleons in his *gousset*, and giving himself no airs at all. He was a better fellow than the one you know perhaps; not that our characters alter, only they develop and our minds grow grey and bald, &c. I was a boy ten years ago, bleating out my simple cries in the Great Hoggarty diamond. We have seen many pretty children, two especially, sitting in a little tub by the roadside; but we agree that there is none so pretty as baby Brookfield, we wish for her

IN THE SCHOOL-ROOM, CLEVEDON COURT.

[From the Clevedon Portraits.]

and for her mother, I believe. This is a brilliant kind of a tour isn't it? egotistical twaddle. I've forgot the lectures as much as if they had never been done, and my impression is that they were a failure. Come along young ladies, we'll go a walk until dinner time, and keep the remainder of this sheet (sacrificing the picture, as after all, why shouldn't we? such a two-penny absurd thing?) and folding the sheet up in a different way. So good bye lady, and I send you a G and a B and a Y.

Lucerne. Monday morning.—We are in love with Berne. We agree that we should like to finish our lives there, it is so homely, charming and beautiful, without knowing it; whereas this place gives itself the airs of a beauty and offends me somehow. We are in an inn like a town, bells begin at four in the morning, two hours ago, and at present all the streets of the hotel are alive; we are not going up the Righi; Y should we go up a dimmed mountain to see a dimmed map under our feet? We are going on to Milan pretty quick. The day after tomorrow we shall sail down the Major lake, we hope to Sesto Calendi and so to Milan. I wonder whether you have written to me to Como? Well, I would have bet five to one on a letter at Berne; but such is life and such is woman, that the philosopher must not reckon on either. And what news would you have sent? that the baby is well, that you have enjoyed yourself pretty well at Sevenoaks? —I would give 6^d to hear as much as that.

[*Here occurs the Drawing reproduced on p.* 150.]
Such is a feeble but accurate outline of the view out of my window at this moment, and all the time I am drawing it, (you will remark how pleasantly the firs and pastures in the foreground are indicated, whereas I cannot do anything with ink, being black, to represent the snow on the mountains behind) I am making pretty dramatic sketches in my mind of misfortune happening to you,—that you are unwell, that you

are thrown out of a carriage, that Dr. Locock is in attendance, *que sais-je?*

As for my dear young ones I am as happy with them as possible; Annie is a fat lump of pure gold, the kindest dearest creature, as well as a wag of the first water. It is an immense blessing that Heaven has given me such an artless affectionate companion. We were looking at a beautiful, smiling, innocent view at Berne, on Saturday, and she said,

And what news w? you have sent? That the baby is well that you have enjoyed yourself pretty well at Sevenoaks? &c. — I would give 6? to hear as much as that. Such is a feeble but accurate outline of the view out of my window at this moment and at the time I am drawing it (you will remark how pleasantly the front fastens in the foreground are with coloured whereas I cant do anything with ink being black to represent the snow on the mountain behind)

"it's like Baby Brookfield." There's for you! and so it was like innocence, and brightness, and &c. &c. Oh! may she never fall in love absurdly and marry an ass! If she will but make her father her confidant, I think the donkey won't long keep his ground in her heart. And so the paper is full and must go to England without ever so much as saying thank you for your letter. Good-bye my dear lady, good-bye Miss Brookfield, Good-bye Mr. Brookfield, says

Your affectionate,

W. M. T.

Au Suisse, July 21st.

[Fragment.] PARIS, 1851.

A Story with a Moral.

Last night I went to a party at the house of my mother's friend Madame Colemache (who introduced me to Madame Ancelot the authoress, who was dying to see me, said Madame Colemache, only I found on talking to Madame Ancelot that she didn't know who I was, and so was no more dying than the most lively of us) and coming down stairs with my Ma I thought to myself, I will go home and have an hour's chat with her, and try and cheer and console her, for her sad tragic looks melted my heart, and always make me think I am a cruel monster; and so I was very tender and sentimental and you see caressed her filially as we went down. It was a wet night and the fly was waiting, and she was just going to step in—but there entered at the house door a fiddler with his fiddle under his arm, whom when dear old *Mater dolorosa* beheld, she said, "O! that is Monsieur *un tel* who has come to play a duo with Laure; I must go back and hear him." And back she went, and all my sentimentality was gulped down and I came home and sent the fly back two miles for her, with Jeames to escort her in the rain. The Moral is that women with those melancholy eyes, and sad, sad looks are not always so melancholy as they seem; they have consolations,—amusements, fiddlers, &c.

. . . . .

I am happy, as happy as I can be here, which is pretty well, though I am bored daily and nightly, and drag about sulkily from tea party to tea party. Last night my mother had her little T, and they danced, and it was not at all unpleasant *quand on y était*. I found an old school-fellow, looking ten years younger than myself, whom I remember older and bigger than myself twenty-eight years ago; and he had got a charming young wife, quite civilized and pleasant to talk to, and the young ladies had their new frocks and looked tolerably respectable, and exceedingly happy. They are to go to a party on Monday, and another on Wednesday, and on Thursday (D. V) we shall be on the homeward road again.

I had cuddled myself with the notion of having one evening to myself, one quiet dinner, one quiet place at the play; but my mother took my only evening and gave it to an old lady whom I don't want to see, and who would have done very well without me,—was there ever such a victim? I go about from house to house and grumble everywhere. I say Thursday, D. V., for what mayn't happen? My poor cousin Charlotte has a relapse of rheumatic fever; my Aunt is in a dreadful prostration and terror. "If anything happens to Charlotte," she says, "I shall die, and then what will Jane do?"

. . . .

There's a kind of glum pleasure, isn't there, in sitting by sick beds and trying to do one's best? I took the old G. P. to dinner at a *Café* yesterday, before the *soirée;* he is very nice and kind and gentle. . . . .

Well, on Wednesday I am going to dine with the Préfet de Police, and afterwards to Madame Scrivanacks ball, where I shall meet,—I, an old fellow of forty—all the pretty actresses of Paris. Let us give a loose to pleasure. . . . .

Mamma and I went to see the old lady last night,—Lady Elgin an honest, grim, big, clever old Scotch lady, well read and good to talk to, dealing in religions of many denominations, and having established in her house as a sort of director, Mr. C. one of the heads of the Irvingites a clever, shifty, sneaking man. I wish I had had your story of Manning; that would have been conversation, but your note didn't arrive till this morning. Thank you, and I hope you are very well. . . . .

I hope you will like good old Miss Agnes Berry; I am sure you will, and shall be glad that you belong to that kind and polite set of old ladies and worthy gentlemen. Mr. Williams too, will approve of them, I should think. I don't know any better company than Foley Wilmot and Poodle Byng. Pass quickly Sunday, Monday, Tuesday, Wednesday. Shall I let Kensington, with ten beds, to an Exhibition-seeing party and live alone? Will you take a lodger who will lend you a fly to go to the parties which you will be continually frequenting? Ah! that would be pleasant.

My cousin Charlotte was much better yesterday, thank God, and her mother quiet. I have been visiting the sick here,—one, two, three, every day. I want to begin to write again very much; my mighty mind is tired of idleness, and ill employs the intervals of rest. . . .

W. M. T.

—— and I are going out for a little ride in half an hour, so that I have plenty of time to send a letter to you. The place here is a neat little thing enough, small and snug, with a great train of *maison* and not more than twenty thousand acres about the house; nothing compared to Gulston, Rumbleberry, Crumply, and most of the places to which one is accustomed, but very well, you understand me, for people of a certain rank of life. One can be happy with many little *désagréments*, when one sees that the people are determined to be civil to one. Nobody here but —— and the Duchess, who don't show at breakfast, and—no, I wont go on writing this dreary nonsense, which was begun before I went out for a long walk and then for a ride. Both were exceedingly pleasant, for there is a beautiful park and gardens and conservatories, and only to see the ducks on the water, and the great big lime trees in the avenue, gives one the keenest sensual pleasure. The wind seemed to me to blow floods of health into my lungs, and the man I was walking with was evidently amused by the excitement and enjoyment of his companion. I recollect His Reverence at Clevedon being surprised at my boyish delight on a similar occasion. It is worth living in London, surely, to enjoy the country when you get to it; and when you go to a man's grounds and get into raptures concerning them, pointing their beauties out with eagerness and feeling, perhaps the host gets a better opinion of his own havings and belongings.

At this juncture I actually fell asleep, being quite tired out with walking, riding, and fresh air. What a gale there is blowing, and what a night your sister must have had to cross! My lady has been uncommonly gracious, and has one of the sweetest voices I ever heard, "an excellent thing in woman." But I am not at my ease yet with her, and tremble rather before her. She is in a great state of suffering, I can see though, and fancy I understand the reason thereof. . . . .

I rode with Lord Ashburton to Alresford, where I heard the magistrates' sessions held, and saw the squires arrive. It was very good fun for me. There was a sentimental case, which somebody would have liked; as handsome a young couple as I ever saw—the girl really beautiful, and the man a deceiver,—and, and,—there was a little baby, and he was condemned to pay 1/6 a week for keeping it; but Lord what it would be to live in that dreary old country town! It is good to see though, and to listen to the squires, and the talk about hunting, and the scandal, and admire the wonderful

[Sketch by Thackeray. (His daughters and Major and Mrs. Carmichael Smyth.) In Mrs. Brookfield's possession.]

varieties of men. We met the little girl and the baby trudging home, sometime afterwards, and the curate in her wake. There seemed no sort of shame about the business, nor love, nor tears, as far as one could see; not a halfpenny worth of romance; only when the child squalled, the mother, who was very fond of it, nursed it, and that made a pretty picture.

What a stupid letter I am writing! I have nothing to say; I left my portmanteau in London, at the station, and was obliged to dine in a frock coat. I hadn't enough clothes to my bed, and couldn't sleep much. . . .   .   .

A Fragment.

FROM THE GRANGE.

The Bishop and a number of clergy are coming here to-morrow and so I stay on for a couple of days. Yesterday it rained without, and I was glad to remain in my room the greater part of the day and to make a good fire and prepare myself for work. But I did none; it wouldn't come—sleep came instead, and between it and the meals and reading Alton Locke—the day passed away. To-day we have had a fine walk—to Trench's parsonage,* a pretty place 3 miles off, through woods of a hundred thousand colours. The Poet was absent but his good-natured wife came to see us; —by Us I mean me, Lady Ashburton, and Miss Farrer, who walked as aide de camp by my lady's pony. How is it that I find myself humbling before her and taking a certain parasitical air as all the rest do? There's something commanding in the woman (she was born in 1806 you'll understand) and I see we all of us bow down before her. Why don't we

* The Rev. R. C. Trench, afterwards Archbishop of Dublin, was at Trinity College with Mr. Thackeray.

bow down before you ma'am. Little Mrs. Taylor is the only one who doesn't seem to Kotoo. I like Taylor,* whose grandeur wears off in ten minutes, and in whom one perceives an extremely gentle and loving human creature I think—not a man to be intimate with ever, but to admire and like from a distance and to have a sort of artistical good will to. . . . We have Carlyle coming down directly the Taylors go away. Major Rawlinson arrives to-night. . . . I've been reading in Alton Locke—Baille Cochrane, Keneally's Goethe— and a book on the decadence of La France proved by figures, and showing that the French are not increasing in wealth or numbers near so fast as the English, Prussians, Russians. Baille Cochrane is an amusing fellow, amusing from his pomposity and historic air ; and Alton Locke begins to be a bore, I think ; and Keneally's Goethe is the work of a mad-cap with a marvellous facility of versifying; and I should like Annie and Minnie to go to my dear lady on Wednesday if you will have them.

* Henry Taylor, author of Philip Van Artevelde,—afterwards Sir Henry Taylor.

1852.

March 18th, 1852, KENSINGTON.

MY DEAR WM.:

I have just received your kind message and melancholy news. Thank you for thinking that I'm interested in what concerns you, and sympathise in what gives you pleasure or grief. Well, I don't think there is much more than this to-day: but I recall what you have said in our many talks of your father, and remember the affection and respect with which you always regarded and spoke of him. Who would wish for more than honour, love, obedience and a tranquil end to old age? And so that generation which engendered us passes away, and their place knows them not; and our turn comes when we are to say good bye to our joys, struggles, pains, affections—and our young ones will grieve and be consoled for us and so on. We've lived as much in 40 as your good old father in his four score years, don't you think so?—and how awfully tired and lonely we are. I picture to myself the placid face of the kind old father with all that trouble and doubt over—his life expiring with supreme blessings for you all—for you and Jane and unconscious little Magdalene prattling and laughing at life's threshold; and know that you will be tenderly cheered and consoled by the good man's blessing for the three of you; while yet, but a minute, but yesterday, but all eternity ago, he was here loving and suffering. I go on with the paper before me—I know there's nothing to say—but I assure you of my sympathy and that I am yours my dear old friend aff'tly,

W. M. THACKERAY.

CLARENDON HOTEL, NEW YORK.
Tuesday, 23 Dec. [1852]

MY DEAR LADY:

I send you a little line and shake your hand across the water. God bless you and yours. . . .

The passage is nothing, now it is over; I am rather ashamed of gloom and disquietude about such a trifling journey. I have made scores of new acquaintances and lighted on my legs as usual. I didn't expect to like people as I do, but am agreeably disappointed and find many most pleasant companions, natural and good; natural and well read and well bred too; and I suppose am none the worse pleased because everybody has read all my books and praises my lectures; (I preach in a Unitarian Church, and the parson comes to hear me. His name is Mr. Bellows, it isn't a pretty name), and there are 2,000 people nearly who come, and the lectures are so well liked that it is probable I shall do them over again. So really there is a chance of making a pretty little sum of money for old age, imbecility, and those young ladies afterwards.

Had Lady Ashburton told you of the moving tables? Try, six or seven of you, a wooden table without brass castors; sit round it, lay your hands flat on it, not touching each other, and in half an hour or so perhaps it will begin to turn round and round. It is the most wonderful thing, but I have tried twice in vain since I saw it and did it at Mr. Bancroft's. I have not been into fashionable society yet, what they call the upper ten thousand here, but have met very likeable of the lower sort. On Sunday I went into the country, and there was a great rosy jolly family of sixteen or eighteen people, round a great tea-table; and the lady of

[From a photograph of Thackeray taken in America, in the possession of Mrs. James T. Fields.]

the house told me to make myself at home—remarking my bashfulness, you know—and said, with a jolly face, and twinkling of her little eyes, " Lord bless you, we know you *all to pieces!*" and there was sitting by me O! such a pretty girl, the very picture of Rubens's second wife, and face and figure. Most of the ladies, all except this family, are as lean as greyhounds; they dress prodigiously fine, taking for their models the French actresses, I think, of the *Boulevard* theatres.

Broadway is miles upon miles long, a rush of life such as I never have seen; not so full as the Strand, but so rapid. The houses are always being torn down and built up again, the railroad cars drive slap into the midst of the city. There are barricades and scaffoldings banging everywhere. I have not been into a house except the fat country one, but something new is being done to it, and the hammerings are clattering in the passage, or a wall, or steps are down, or the family is going to move. Nobody is quiet here, no more am I. The rush and restlessness pleases me, and I like, for a little, the dash of the stream. I am not received as a god, which I like too. There is one paper which goes on every morning saying I am a snob, and I don't say no. Six people were reading it at breakfast this morning, and the man opposite me popped it under the table cloth. But the other papers roar with approbation. "*Criez, beuglez O! Journaux*" They don't understand French though, that bit of Béranger will hang fire. Do you remember *Jété sur cette boule* &c.? Yes, my dear sister remembers. God Almighty bless her, and all she loves.

I may write next Saturday to Chesham Place; you will go and carry my love to those ladies won't you? Here comes in a man with a paper I hadn't seen; I must cut out a bit just as the actors do, but then I think you will like it, and that is why I do it. There was a very rich biography about me in one of the papers the other day, with an account of a servant, maintained in the splendour of his menial decorations —Poor old John whose picture is in *Pendennis*. And I have filled my paper, and I shake my dear lady's hand across the roaring sea, and I know that you will be glad to know that I prosper and that I am well, and that I am yours

W. M. T.

[*Cutting from the New York Evening Post enclosed in the foregoing.*]

The building was crowded to its utmost capacity with the celebrities of literature and fashion in this metropolis, all of whom, we believe, left, perfectly united in the opinion that they never remembered to have spent an hour more delightfully in their lives, and that the room in which they had been receiving so much enjoyment, was very badly lighted. We fear, also, that it was the impression of the many who were disappointed in getting tickets, that the room was not spacious enough for the purpose in which it has been appropriated.

Every one who saw Mr. Thackeray last evening for the first, seemed to have had their impressions of his appearance and manner of speech, corrected. Few expected to see so large a man; he is gigantic, six feet four at least; few expected to see so old a person; his hair appears to have kept silvery record over fifty years; and then there was a notion in the minds of many that there must be something dashing and "fast" in his appearance, whereas his costume was perfectly plain; the expression of his face grave and earnest; his address perfectly unaffected, and such as we might expect to meet with, in a well bred man somewhat advanced in years.

His elocution, also, surprised those who had derived their impressions from the English journals. His voice is a superb tenor, and possesses that pathetic tremble which is so effective in what is called emotive eloquence, while his delivery was as well suited to the communication he had to make as could well have been imagined.

His enunciation is perfect. Every word he uttered might have been heard in the remotest quarters of the room, yet he scarcely lifted his voice above a colloquial tone. The most striking feature in his whole manner was the utter absence of affectation of any kind. He did not permit himself to appear conscious that he was an object of peculiar interest in the audience, neither was he guilty of the greater error of not appearing to care whether they were interested in him or not. In other words, he inspired his audience with a respect for him, as a man proportioned to the admiration, which his books have inspired for him as an author.

Of the lecture itself, as a work of art, it would be difficult to speak too strongly. Though written with the utmost simplicity and apparent inattention to effects, it overflowed with every characteristic of the author's happiest vein. There has been nothing written about Swift so clever, and if we except Lord Orrery's silly letters, we suspect we might add nothing so unjust.

Though suitable credit was given to Swift's talents, all of which were admirably characterized, yet when he came to speak of the moral side of the dean's nature he saw nothing but darkness.

1853.

Direct Clarendon Hotel New York.

        PHILADELPHIA.
        21 to 23 January.

 My dear lady's kind sad letter gave me pleasure, melancholy as it was. . . .

 At present, I incline to come to England in June or July and get ready a new set of lectures, and bring them back with me. That second course will enable me to provide for the children and their mother finally and satisfactorily, and my mind will be easier after that, and I can sing *Nunc Dimittis* without faltering. There is money-making to try at, to be sure, and ambition,—I mean in public life; perhaps that might interest a man, but not novels, nor lectures, nor fun, any more. I don't seem to care about these any more, or for praise, or for abuse, or for reputation of that kind. That literary play is played out, and the puppets going to be locked up for good and all.

 Does this melancholy come from the circumstance that I have been out to dinner and supper every night this week? O! I am tired of shaking hands with people, and acting the lion business night after night. Everybody is introduced and shakes hands. I know thousands of Colonels, professors, editors, and what not, and walk the streets guiltily, knowing that I don't know 'em, and trembling lest the man opposite to me is one of my friends of the day before. I believe I am popular, except at Boston among the newspaper men who fired into me, but a great favorite with the *monde* there and elsewhere. Here in Philadelphia it is all praise and kindness. Do you know there are 500,000 people in Philadelphia? I daresay you had no idea thereof, and smile at the idea of there being a *monde* here and at Boston and New York. Early next month I begin at Washington and Baltimore, then D. V. to New Orleans, back to New York by Mississippi and Ohio, if the steamers don't blow up, and if they do, you know I am easy. What a weary, weary letter I am writing to you. . . . Have you heard that I have found Beatrix at New York? I have basked in her bright eyes, but Ah, me! I don't care for her, and shall hear of her marrying a New York buck with a feeling of perfect pleasure. She is really as like Beatrix, as that fellow William and I met was like Costigan. She has a dear woman of a mother upwards of fifty-five, whom I like the best, I think, and think the handsomest,—a sweet lady. What a comfort those dear Elliots are to me; I have had but one little letter from J. E. full of troubles too. She says you have been a comfort to them too. I can't live without the tenderness of some woman; and expect when I am sixty I shall be marrying a girl of eleven or twelve, innocent, barley-sugar-loving, in a pinafore.

They came and interrupted me as I was writing this, two days since; and I have been in public almost ever since. The lectures are enormously *suivies* and I read at the rate of a pound a minute nearly. The curious thing is, that I think I improve in the reading; at certain passages a sort of emotion springs up, I begin to understand how actors feel affected over and over again at the same passages of the play; —they are affected off the stage too, I hope I shan't be.

Crowe is my immensest comfort; I could not live without someone to take care of me, and he is the kindest and most affectionate henchman ever man had. I went to see Pierce Butler yesterday, Fanny's husband. I thought she would like me to see the children if I could, and I asked about them particularly, but they were not shown. I thought of good Adelaide coming to sing to you when you were ill. I may like everyone who is kind to you, mayn't I? . . .

What for has Lady Ashburton never written to me? I am writing this with a new gold pen in such a fine gold case. An old gentleman gave it to me yesterday, a white-headed old philosopher and political economist. There's something simple in the way these kind folks regard a man; they read our books as if we were Fielding, and so forth. The other night some men were talking of Dickens and Bulwer as if they were equal to Shakespeare, and I was pleased to find myself pleased at hearing them praised. The prettiest girl in Philadelphia, poor soul, has read *Vanity Fair* twelve times. I paid her a great big compliment yesterday, about her good looks of course, and she turned round delighted to her friend and said, "*Ai most tallut,*" that is something like the pronunciation. Beatrix has an adorable pronunciation, and uses little words, which are much better than wit. And what do you think? One of the prettiest girls in Boston is to be put under my charge to go to a marriage at Washington next week. We are to travel together all the way alone—only, only, I'm not going. Young people when they are engaged here, make tours alone; fancy what the British Mrs. Grundy would say at such an idea!

There was a young quakeress at the lecture last night, listening about Fielding. Lord! Lord. how pretty she was! There are hundreds of such everywhere, airy looking little beings, with magnolia—no not magnolia, what is that white flower you make bouquets of, camilla or camelia—complexions, and lasting not much longer. . . . God bless you and your children, write to me sometimes and farewell.

[*To Miss Perry*].

BALTIMORE,—WASHINGTON.

Feby. 7th. to 14th. '53.

Although I have written a many letters to Chesham Place not one has gone to the special address of my dear K. E. P., and if you please I will begin one now for half an hour before going to lecture 1. In another hour that dreary business of "In speaking of the English Humourous writers of the last, etc." will begin,—and the wonder to me is that the speaker once in the desk (to-day it is to be a right down pulpit in a Universalist Church and no mistake), gets interested in the work, makes the points, thrills with emotion and indignation at the right place, and has a little sensation whilst the work is going on; but I can't go on much longer, my conscience revolts at the quackery. Now I have seen three great cities, Boston, New York, Philadelphia, I think I like them all mighty well they seem to me not so civilized as our London, but more so than Manchester and Liverpool. At Boston is very good literate company indeed; it is like Edinburgh for that,—a vast amount of toryism and donnishness everywhere. That of New York the simplest and least pretentious; it suffices that a man should keep a fine house, give parties, and have a daughter, to get all the world to him. And what struck me, that whereas on my first arrival, I was annoyed at the uncommon splendatiousness

—here the letter was interrupted on Monday at Baltimore, and is now taken up again on Thursday at Washington—never mind what struck me, it was only that after a while you get accustomed to the splendor of the dresses and think them right and proper. Use makes everything so;

who knows? you will be coming out in Empire ruffs and high waists by the time I come home. I have not been able to write a word since I came here on Tuesday; my time has been spent in seeing and calling upon lions. Our minister Mr. Crampton is very jolly and good-natured. Yesterday he had a dinner at five for all the legation, and they all came very much bored to my lecture. To-day I dined with Mr. Everett; with the President it may be next week. The place has a Wiesbaden air—there are politics and gaieties straggling all over it. More interruption and this one has lasted three days. Book indeed! How is one to write a book when it is next to impossible to get a quiet half hour? Since I wrote has come a short kind letter from dear old Kinglake, who continues to give bad accounts from Chesham Place. God bless all there, say I. I wish I was by to be with my dear friends in grief, I know they know how to sympathize (although we are spoiled by the world, we have no hearts you know &c. &c.; but then it may happen that the high flown romantic people are wrong, and that we love our friends as well as they do). I don't pity anybody who leaves the world, not even a fair young girl in her prime; I pity those remaining. On her journey, if it pleases God to send her, depend on it there's no cause for grief, that's but an earthly condition. Out of our stormy life, and brought nearer the Divine light and warmth, there must be a serene climate. Can't you fancy sailing into the calm? Would you care about going on the voyage, only for the dear souls left on the other shore? but we shan't be parted from them no doubt though they are from us. Add a little more intelligence to that which we possess even as we are, and why shouldn't we be with our friends though ever so far off? . .

. Why presently, the body removed, shouldn't we personally be anywhere at will—properties of Creation, like the electric something (spark is it?) that thrills all round the

globe simultaneously? and if round the globe why not *Über-
all?* and the body being removed or else where disposed of
and developed, sorrow and its opposite, crime and the re-
verse, ease and disease, desire and dislike &c. go along with
the body—a lucid Intelligence remains, a Perception ubiqui-
tous. *Monday.* I was interrupted a dozen times yesterday
in the course of these profitless *Schwärmereien.*—There's
no rest here for pilgrims like me. Have I told you on the
other side that I'm doing a good business at Baltimore and a
small select one here? the big-wigs all come and are pleased;
all the legations and old Scott the unsuccessful candidate for
the Presidency &c.? It is well to have come. I shall go
hence to Richmond and Charleston and then who knows
whither? not to New Orleans, I think the distance is too
great. I can't go a thousand miles fishing for half as many
pounds. Why not come back and see all the dear faces at
home? I try and think of something to say about this country; all I have remarked I could put down in two pages.
Where's the eager observation and ready pencil of five years
ago? I have not made a single sketch. The world passes
before me and I don't care—Is it a weary heart or is it a
great cold I have got in my nose which stupefies me utterly?
I won't inflict any more megrims upon you,

from your affectionate friend and
brother

W. M. T.

[*To Mrs. Elliot and her sister Miss Perry.*]

March 3rd. 1853.
RICHMOND, VIRGINIA.

Address the
    Clarendon—New York.

Fragment.

I am getting so sick and ashamed of the confounded old lectures that I wonder I have the courage to go on delivering them. I shan't read a single review of them when they are published; anything savage said about them will serve them right. They are popular enough here. The two presidents at Washington came to the last, and in this pretty little town the little Atheneum Hall was crowded so much that its a pity I had not hired a room twice as big; but £2500 is all I shall make out of them. Well that is £200 a year in this country and an immense comfort for the chicks.—Crowe has just come out from what might have been and may be yet a dreadful scrape. He went into a slave market and began sketching; and the people rushed on him savagely and obliged him to quit. Fancy such a piece of imprudence. It may fall upon his chief, who knows, and cut short his popularity.

The negroes don't shock me, or excite my compassionate feelings at all; they are so grotesque and happy that I can't cry over them. The little black imps are trotting and grinning about the streets, women, workmen, waiters, all well fed and happy. The place the merriest little place and the most picturesque I have seen in America, and on Saturday I go to Charlestown—shall I go thence to Havannah? who knows.

I should like to give myself a week's holiday, without my demd lecture box. Shake every one by the hand that asks about me.

I am yours always—O! you kind friends——
W. M. T.

[*To Miss Perry*].

SAVANNAH, GEORGIA,—[1855]
Feast of St. Valentine.

This welcome day brought me a nice long letter from K. E. P., and she must know that I write from the most comfortable quarters I have ever had in the United States. In a tranquil old city, wide-streeted, tree-planted, with a few cows and carriages toiling through the sandy road, a few happy negroes sauntering here and there, a red river with a tranquil little fleet of merchant-men taking in cargo, and tranquil ware-houses barricaded with packs of cotton,—no row, no tearing northern bustle, no ceaseless hotel racket, no crowds drinking at the bar,—a snug little languid audience of three or four hundred people, far too lazy to laugh or applaud; a famous good dinner, breakfast etc, and leisure all the morning to think and do and sleep and read as I like. The only place I say in the States where I can get these comforts—all free gratis—is in the house of my friend Andrew Low of the great house of A. Low and Co., Cotton Dealers, brokers, Merchants—what's the word? Last time I was here he was a widower with two daughters in England, about whom—and other two daughters—there was endless talk between us. Now there is a pretty wife added to the establishment, and a little daughter number three crowing in the adjoining nursery. They are tremendous men these cotton merchants.

When I had finished at Charleston I went off to a queer little rustic city called Augusta—a great broad street 2 miles long—old quaint looking shops—houses with galleries—ware-houses—trees—cows and negroes strolling about the side walks—plank roads—a happy dirty tranquility generally prevalent. It lies 130 miles from Charleston. You take 8½ hours to get there by the railway, about same time and distance to come here, over endless plains of swampy pine-lands—a village or two here and there in a clearing. I brought away a snug little purse from snug little Augusta, though I had a rival—A Wild man, lecturing in the very same hall: I tell you it is not a dignified *métier*, that which I pursue.

What is this about the *Saturday Review?* After giving Vernon Harcourt 2/6 to send me the first 5 numbers, and only getting No. 1, it is too bad they should assault me—and for what? My lecture is rather extra loyal whenever the Queen is mentioned,—and the most applauded passage in them I shall have the honour of delivering to-night in the Lecture on George II, where the speaker says " In laughing at these old-world follies and ceremonies shall we not acknowledge the change of to-day? As the mistress of St. James passes me now I salute the sovereign, wise, moderate, exemplary of life, the good mother, the good wife, the accomplished Lady, the enlightened friend of Art, the tender sympathizer in her people's glories and sorrows."

I can't say more, can I? and as for George III, I leave off just with the people on the crying point. And I never for one minute should think that my brave old Venables would hit me; or if he did that he hadn't good cause for it.

Forster's classification delights me. It's right that men of such ability and merit should get government recognition and honourable public employ. It is a compliment to all of us when one receives such promotion. As for me I have pestered you with my account of dollars and cents, and it is quite clear that Kings or Laws cannot do anything so well for me as these jaws and this pen—please God they are allowed to wag a little longer. I wish I did not read about your illness and weakness in that letter. Ah, me! many and many a time every day do I think of you all.

Enter a servant (black) with the card of Bishop Elliott.. . . . .

If you are taking a drive some day, do go and pay a visit of charity to my good cook and house-keeper Gray, and say you have heard of me, and that I am very well and making plenty of money and that Charles is well and is the greatest comfort to me. It will comfort the poor woman all alone in poor 36 yonder. What charming letters Annie writes me with exquisite pretty turns now and then. St. Valentine brought me a delightful letter from her too, and from the dear old mother; and whether it's the comfort of this house, or the pleasure of having an hour's chat with you, or the sweet clean bed I had last night and undisturbed rest and good breakfast, —altogether I think I have no right to grumble at my lot and am very decently happy, don't you?

16th Feb. My course is for Macon, Montgomery and New Orleans; no Havannah, the dollars forbid. From N. O. I shall go up the Mississippi, D. V., to St. Louis and Cincinnati, and ye who write will address care of J. G. King's Sons, New York, won't you?

Yours afft.
W. M. T.

AN IMAGINARY LETTER FROM NEW YORK.*

September 5, 1848.

DEAR MADAM:—

It seems to me a long time since I had the honour of seeing you. I shall be glad to have some account of your health. We made a beautiful voyage of 13½ days, and reached this fine city yesterday. The entrance of the bay is beautiful; magnificent woods of the Susquehannah stretch down to the shore, and from Hoboken lighthouse to Vancouver's Island, the bay presents one brilliant blaze of natural and commercial loveliness. Hearing that Titmarsh was on board the steamer, the Lord Mayor and Aldermen of New York came down to receive us, and the batteries on Long Island fired a salute. General Jackson called at my hotel, (the Astor house) I found him a kind old man, though he has a wooden leg and takes a great deal of snuff. Broadway has certainly disappointed me —it is nothing to be compared to our own dear Holborn Hill. But the beautiful range of the Allegheney mountains, which I see from my windows, and the roar of the Niagara Cataract, which empties itself out of the Mississippi into the Oregon territory, have an effect, which your fine eye for the picturesque, and keen sense of the beautiful and the natural would I am sure lead you to appreciate.

The oysters here are much larger than ours, and the canvass backed ducks, are reckoned, and indeed are, a delicacy. The house where Washington was born is still shown, but the General I am informed, is dead, much regretted. The

---

* This letter, the only one of those in the collection which has been made public before, was printed by permission in the *Orphan of Pimlico*, a little collection of Thackeray's *miscellanea* and drawings published in 1876. As it will be new to most readers, however, it has been thought best to retain it; and it is placed here simply to be in company with the real American letters. The drawing of the Negro, however, which accompanied it also in the *Orphan of Pimlico*, seems to have been an actual sketch during one of the American visits.

clergy here is both numerous and respected, and the Archbishop of New York is a most venerable and delightful prelate; whose sermons are however a little long. The ladies are without exception the—But here the first gong sounds for dinner, and the black slave who waits on me, comes up and says, " Massa, hab only five minutes for dinnah." " Make haste, git no pumpkin pie else," so unwillingly I am obliged to break off my note and to subscribe myself,

       My dear Madame
          Your very faithful servt.,
             W. M. THACKERAY.

[1854]

I hope you will not object to hear that I am quite well this morning. I should have liked to shake hands with H. before his departure, but I was busy writing at the hour when he said he was going, and fell sound asleep here last night, after a very modest dinner, not waking till near midnight, when it was too late to set off to the Paddington Station.

What do you think I have done to-day? I have sent in my resignation to *Punch*. There appears in next *Punch* an article, so wicked, I think, by poor ——— that upon my word I don't think I ought to pull any longer in the same boat with such a savage little Robespierre. The appearance of this incendiary article put me in such a rage, that I could only cool myself by a ride in the Park; and I should very likely have reported myself in Portman Street, but I remembered how you had Miss Prince to luncheon, and how I should be *de trop*. Now I am going to work the rest of the middle of the day until dinner time, when I go to see *Le Prophète* again; but it would please me very much, if you please, to hear that you were pretty well.

Always faithfully *de Madame le serviteur dévoué*

W. M. T.

The letters which have been chosen for publication end here. During the many years that they have remained in my possession no one has read them out of my own family, with the exception of Mr. Thackeray's beloved daughter, Mrs. Ritchie; until these last few months, when two or three of these letters were read by the friends whom I consulted as to their suitability for publication. As my own life draws to a close, I still look back to the confidence and affection with which their writer honoured me, with gratitude too deep for words. The record of these few years of his life, given by his own hand in every varied mood, will best describe him as he was and as I so well remember him; but my friend Kate Perry's charming recollections cannot fail to be read with general interest.

JANE OCTAVIA BROOKFIELD.

∗∗ In addition to the passages quoted from Miss Perry, I give two slight anecdotes of my own early acquaintance:

When, soon after our marriage, Mr. Brookfield introduced his early college friend, Mr. Thackeray, to me, he brought him one day unexpectedly to dine with us. There was, fortunately, a good plain dinner, but I was young and shy enough to feel embarrassed because we had no sweets, and I privately sent my maid to the nearest confectioner's to buy a dish of tartlets, which I thought would give a finish to our simple meal. When they were placed before me, I timidly offered our guest a small one, saying, 'Will you have a tartlet, Mr. Thackeray?' 'I will, but I'll have a two-penny one, if you please,' he answered, so beamingly, that we all laughed, and my shyness disappeared.

On another occasion, also very early in my friendship with Mr. Thackeray, he was at our house one evening with a few other intimate friends, when the conversation turned on court circulars, and their sameness day after day. A few samples were given: 'So-and-so had the honor of joining Her Majesty's dinner party with other lofty and imposing personages,' invariably ending with Dr. Pretorius. 'By the way, who is Dr. Pretorius?' somebody asked. A slight pause ensued, when a voice began solemnly singing the National Anthem, ending each verse with,

> " God save our gracious Queen,
>   Send her victorious, happy and glorious,
>   Dr. Pretorius—God save the Queen."

This was Mr. Thackeray, who had been sitting perfectly silent and rather apart from those who were talking, and had not appeared to notice what was said.

SOME EXTRACTS FROM MISS KATE PERRY'S RECOLLECTIONS OF MR. THACKERAY.

My acquaintance with Mr. Thackeray began at Brighton, where I was staying with my eldest brother, William Perry. In most cases there is a prelude to friendship—at first it is a delicate plant, with barely any root, gradually throwing out tender green leaves and buds, and then full-blown flowers— the root in the meanwhile taking firm hold of the earth—and cruel is the frost or cutting wind which destroys it. But Mr. Thackeray and I went through no gradations of growth in our friendship; it was more like Jack's bean-stalk in a pantomime, which rushed up sky-high without culture, and, thank God, so remained till his most sad and sudden end.

In the earliest days of our friendship he brought his morning work to read to me in the evening; he had just commenced "Vanity Fair," and was living at the Old Ship Inn, where he wrote some of the first numbers. He often then said to me: "I wonder whether this will take, the publishers accept it, and the world read it?" I remember answering him that I had no reliance upon my own critical powers in literature; but that I had written to my sister, Mrs. Frederick Elliot, and said, "I have made a great friendship with one of the principal contributors of *Punch*—Mr. Thackeray; he is now writing a novel, but cannot hit upon a name for it. I may be wrong, but it seems to me the cleverest thing I ever read. The first time he dined with us I was fearfully alarmed at him. The next day we walked in Chichester Park, when he told all about his little girls, and of his great friendship with the Brookfields, and I told him about you and Chesham Place." When he heard this, and my opinion of his novel, he burst out laughing, and said: "Ah! Mademoiselle (as he always called me), it is *not* small beer; but I do not know whether it will be palatable to the London folks." He told me, some time afterward, that, after ransacking his brain for a name for his novel, it came upon him unawares, in the middle of the night, as if a voice had whispered, "Vanity Fair." He said, "I jumped out of bed, and ran three times round my room, uttering as I went, 'Vanity Fair, Vanity Fair, Vanity Fair.'"

Afterward we frequently met at the Miss Berrys', where night after night were assembled all the wit and beauty of that time. There was such a charm about these gatherings of friends, that hereafter we may say: "There is no salon now to compare to that of the Miss Berrys', in Curzon Street." My sister and I, with our great admiration and friendship for Mr. Thackeray, used to think that the Miss Berrys at first did not thoroughly appreciate or understand

[From an etching of a portrait by Samuel Lawrence.]

him; but one evening, when he had left early, they said they had perceived, for the first time, "what a very remarkable man he was." He became a constant and most welcome visitor at their house; they read his works with delight, and, whenever they were making up a pleasant dinner, used to say: "We *must* have Thackeray." It was at one of these dinners that Miss Berry astonished us all by saying she "had never read Jane Austen's novels, until lately someone had lent them to her. But she could not get on with them; they were totally uninteresting to her—long-drawn-out details of very ordinary people," and she found the books so tedious that she could not understand their having obtained such a celebrity as they had done. "Thackeray and Balzac," she added (Thackeray being present), "write with great minuteness, but do so with a brilliant pen." Thackeray made two bows of gratitude (one, pointing to the ground, for Balzac). Those who love to pore over old memoirs will find Miss Berry's name associated with Horace Walpole's; but when they met he was very old, and she was very young. She accepted his admiration with pride and gratitude, but had no aspiration to be the mistress of Strawberry Hill.

Miss Agnes Berry adored her elder sister; *she* had considerable clearness and acuteness of perception, and Thackeray always maintained she was the more naturally gifted of the two sisters. In her youth she was a pretty, charming girl, with whom Gustavus Adolphus danced at one of his court balls, and was admired and envied by the other ladies present. These two remarkable women lived together for nearly ninety years.

Thackeray's love of children was one of the strongest feelings of his heart. In a little poem, "The Golden Pen," pubished in his "Miscellanies," which is, perhaps, the truest portrait of him which has ever appeared, he writes:

> "There's something, even in his bitterest mood,
> That melts him at the sight of infanthood;
> Thank God that he can love the pure and good."

This sympathy with the little ones was not only proved by his immense devotion to his own most gifted children, but extended to the little "gutter child," as the trim board-school girl of to-day was called then. For this waif of society he felt the tenderest pity and interest. He used often to visit a school where my dear sister had collected nearly three hundred of these neglected children, feeding, teaching, and clothing them, and, with the help of other kind souls, preparing them in some degree to fight the battle of life, in which there are many crosses—but few Victoria ones. Turning his steps one day to this large, rough-looking school-room, he entered it just as these little Arabs were commencing, with more heartiness than melody, Faber's beautiful hymn:

> "O Paradise! O Paradise!
> Who doth not crave for rest?
> Who would not seek the happy land,
> Where they that love are blest?"

He turned to the lady superintending them, and said, "I cannot stand this any longer—my spectacles are getting very dim."

One day, some few years later, I had been engaged in summing up the monthly expenses of the same school, and had left open on my writing-table, the much scored-over Soup Kitchen book. Mr. Thackeray was shown into the room, and was for some minutes alone before I joined him. After he left, I resumed my labors, and found on the first page of the book a beautifully executed pen-and-ink sketch of little children crowding round the school-mistress, who was ladling out, into mugs of various sizes and shapes, the daily meal of soup, above which was written, "Suffer little children, and forbid them not."

Another day, I found a sovereign under a paper containing the names of some friends of the school who had joined in a subscription to give the children a day's holiday in the country. I said to my servant, "Mr. Thackeray has been here," and found from him this was the case. I knew my instinct was right, that it was his hand which had placed the money there. His charity was very wide, in the fullest sense of the word. He has been known to discover, in some remote corner, the hapless artist or dramatist who in his palmy days had not thought much of that night—old age—"when no more work can be done." Thackeray would mount the many steps leading to the desolate chamber—administer some little rebuke on the thoughtlessness of not laying by some of the easily gained gold of youth or manhood, and slipping, as in one instance, into an old blotting-book, a £100 note, would hurry away.

"I never saw him do it," said poor old P——. "I was very angry because he said I had been a reckless old goose—and then a £100 falls out of my writing-book. God bless him!"

These good deeds would never have come to light but for the gratitude of those who, though they had the gentle rebuke, received also the more than liberal help. I know he has been accused of extreme sensitiveness to blame, either about himself or his writings, but the following story proves that he could forgive with magnanimity and grace when roughly and severely handled. This once occurred at my sister's dinner-table. Thackeray, who was almost a daily visitor at her house, for some time took it into his head, to be announced by the name of the most noted criminal of the day. Our butler did this with the greatest gravity.

On this occasion Thackeray had been asked to join some friends at dinner, but not arriving at the prescribed hour, the guests sat down without him. Among them was Mr. H——, the author of some of the most charming books of the day.

The conversation being more literary than otherwise, Thackeray (then at the very height of his fame) came under discussion, and, some of his greatest friends and admirers being present, he was spoken of with unqualified admiration. Mr. H—— was the exception, and dissented from us, in very unmeasured terms, in our estimate of Thackeray's character. Judging, he said, "from the tenor of his books, he could not believe how one who could dwell, as he did, on the weakness and absurdities and shortcomings of his fellow-creatures, could possess any kind or generous sympathies toward the human race." He concluded his severe judgment by saying that, "He had never met him, and hoped he never should do so."

We were all so occupied by this fiery debate that we did not observe that, under the sobriquet of some jail-bird of the day, Thackeray had slipped into his chair, and heard much that was said, including the severe peroration. A gentle tap on Mr. H——'s shoulder, and, in his pleasant, low voice, Thackeray said, "I, on the contrary, have always longed for the occasion when I could express, personally, to Mr. H——, the great admiration I have always felt for him, as an author and a man." It is pleasant to think they became fast friends thereafter.

NOTE.—The little sketch of the cupid [p. 183] was sent to Miss Perry unfinished as it is, as an acknowledgment for some grapes which she had given to one of his daughters who was not well. J. O. B.

I find it difficult to check my pen from being garrulous as I remember the many instances of the kindness and generosity of his nature, though, at the same time, I feel how inadequate it is to do justice to all his noble and delightful qualities. His wit and humor and playfulness were most observable where he was happiest and most at ease,—with his beloved daughters, or with his dear friends the Brookfields, who were the most intimate and valued of those he made in middle life. I am proud to say, also, that he was aware of the admiration in which he was held by every member of my sister's home, where his ever ready sympathy in all our troubles and pleasures was truly appreciated—and when he passed away, and the place knew him no more, a great shadow fell upon that house.

KATE PERRY.

INDEX.

[*All letters not especially addressed to others were written to Mrs. Brookfield, or Mr. and Mrs. Brookfield jointly.*]

AINSWORTH, W. H., 84.
　Alexis, the somnambulist, 56, 57.
Alresford, the magistrate's sessions at, 154.
Ancelot, Mme., 151.
Arlincourt, Vicomte d', 114.
Ashburton, Lord, 154.
Ashburton, Lady, 36, 58, 67, 97, 155, 158.

BALTIMORE, Thackeray at, 165.
Beauvoir, Roger de, 88.
Bedford, the Dowager Duchess of, 53.
Bellows, Rev. Henry W., 158.
Benedict, Sir Julius, 59 *n.*
Berne, Thackeray at, 147.
Berry, the Misses, 47, 67, 99, 104, 178.
Blenheim, Thackeray at, 31.
Bonneval, Mme. de, 146.
Bracebridge, Mr. and Mrs., 22.
Brandauer, Miss, 24.
Brighton, Thackeray at, 61.
Brohan, Mlle., 80.
Brookfield, Rev. William Henry (often referred to in the letters by various names, as "Mr. Williams," "the Inspector," etc.), 7 *n.*, 23, 25, 26, 33, 36, 37, 42, 44, 48, 50, 60 *et seq.*, 67, 76, 85, 86, 87, 92, 101, 108, 114, 117, 118, 125 ; letters to, 5, 6, 8, 22, 27, 28, 30, 51, 54, 58, 59, 70, 129, 135, 136, 137, 157.
Brougham, Lord, 99.
Brussels, Thackeray at, 9 *et seq.*
Budd, Captain, 46.
Bullar, Joseph, 22, 35, 89.
Bullar, William, 139.
Buller, Charles, death of, 33.
Butler, Pierce, 163.
Byng, Mr., 153.

CANTERBURY, Thackeray at, 10.
Carlyle, Thomas, 34, 116, 156.
Castlereagh, Lord and Lady, 103, 107, 114, 123.
Chapman, Mr., 10.
Chasles, Mr., 77.
Chronicle, The, Thackeray's contributions to, 29.
Clevedon Court, 7 *n.*, 28 *n.*, 30.
Colemache, Mme., 151.
Cowper, Spencer, 56.
Crampton, Mr., British Minister at Washington, 166.
Crowe, Eyre, 58 *n.*

Crowe, Mr., 6.
Crowe, Mrs., 58 *n*., 67.
Crowe, Thackeray's servant, 163.

DAMER, Colonel, 104.
"David Copperfield," 54, 87.
Davy, Lady, 46, 15.
De Bathe, Sir Henry and Lady, 59.
Dejazet, Mlle., 14.
Dickens, Charles, "Reconciliation banquet" given to him and Thackeray by Forster, 5; Letter of A. H. concerning, with Thackeray's comments, 7; Thackeray on, 68.
Dilke, Charles Wentworth, 29.
Dover, Thackeray at, 11, 37.
Doyle, Richard, 133.

ELGIN, Lady, 152.
Ellice, Mr., 107.
Elliot, Frederick, 142.
Elliot, Mrs., 103, 128, 141; letters to, 168 *et seq*., 178.
Elliot, Miss Hatty, 104.
Elliotson, Dr., 73, 103.
Elton, Sir Charles, 7 *n*., 28 *n*.
Elton, Sir Edmund, 28 *n*.
Errington, Mrs., 79.
Evening Post, The, New York, Extract from, on Thackeray's lectures, 160.
Everett, Edward, 166.
Exhibition of 1851, 134.

FARRER, Miss, 155.
Fanshawe, Mrs., 48, 79.
Fielding's Novels, Thackeray on, 120.

Fonblanque, Mr., 66.
Forster, John, His "reconciliation banquet," 5; mention of, 10 and *n*.
Fraser, Thomas, 79.

GALIGNANI'S MESSENGER, Thackeray's contributions to, 36.
Gigoux, Mr., 108.
Gordon, Sir Alexander and Lady Duff, 59.
Granville, Lady, 53.
Gudin, Théodore, 108.
Gudin, Mme., 80, 113.

HALLAM, Henry Fitzmaurice, 29, 30, 59, 128; death of, 129.
Hallam, Miss, 69.
Halliday, Mr., 79.
Heidelberg, Thackeray at, 145.
Herbert, Mrs., 125.
Higgins, Matthew James (Jacob Omnium), 67 *n*.
Hislop, Lady, 104.
Holland, Lord, 131.
Hôtel des Pays Bas, Spa, 16 *et seq*.
Howden, Lord, 105.

JACOBS, the Wizard, 11.
"Jane Eyre," its authorship attributed to Procter, 29.
Janin, Jules, 74 *et seq*.
Jones, Longueville, 36.

KENYON, Mr., 129.
Kinglake, Alexander William, 104.
Kingsley, Charles, 145.

INDEX.

LAMARTINE, Alphonse de, 38.
Lansdowne, Lord, 116.
Leslie, the Misses, 53.
Lind, Mme. Jennie, 59, 119.
Literary Fund, Thackeray's dinner and speech at, 120 *et seq.*
Louvre, the, Thackeray at, 77.
Lovelace, Lady, 47.
Low, Andrew, 169.
Lucerne, Thackeray at, 149.
Lytton, Sir Bulwer, 123.

MACAULAY, Thomas Babington, 90, 92.
Macdonald, Norman, 33.
Mackenzie, Mrs. Stewart, 144.
Maine, Henry, 117.
Marrast, Mr., 38.
Martchenko, Mr., 146.
Meurice's Hotel, Paris, Thackeray at, 38.
Mill, John Stuart, 98.
Molesworth, Sir William and Lady, 127.
Montgomery, Mrs. Alfred, 70, 71.
Morgan, Captain, 53.
Morier, Mr., 34, 63.
Morley, Lady, 116.
"Mystères de Londres," a French play, Thackeray's description of, 40.

NAPIER, Sir George, 92.
New York, Thackeray in, 158; imaginary letter from, 172.
Normanby, Lord, 39, 107.

O'BRIEN, Smith, 19.
Orsay, the Count d', 111.

Osy, Mme., 80.
Oxford, Thackeray at, 31.

PALMER, Mr., 62.
Paris, Thackeray in, 38, 74 *et seq.*, 104 *et seq.*, 151 *et seq.*
Parr, Mrs., 30, 72.
Parr, Thomas, 144.
Pattle, Miss Virginia, 65 *n.*, 97, 128.
Payne, Mrs. Brookfield's maid, 20, 23.
Peacock, Thomas Love, 100.
Peel, Sir Robert and Lady, 116.
"Pendennis," 27, 29, 42, 46, 48, 49, 63, 65, 67, 74, 84, 97.
Perry, Miss Kate, 55, 103; her recollections of Thackeray, 177; letters to, 168, 169.
Perry, William, 177.
Philadelphia, Thackeray in, 162.
Powell, Mrs., 70.
Prinsep, Mr. and Mrs., 65 *n.*, 97.
Procter, Adelaide, 29, 47, 70.
Procter, Bryan Waller (Barry Cornwall), 44, 45 *n.*
Procter, Mrs., 27, 49, 53, 54, 126.
Punch, 25; Thackeray resigns from, 174.

ROTHESAY, Lady Stuart de, 104.
Rawlinson, Major, 156.
Rehda, baths of, 22.
Rice, Spring, 136.
Richmond, Thackeray at, 168.
Robbins, Mrs., 72.
Rothschild, Baron, 38.
Royal Scots Fusiliers, Thackeray's visit to, 10.
Ryde, Thackeray at, 54.

SANDWICH, Lady, 107.
  Sartoris, Mrs., 61.
Savannah, Thackeray at, 169.
Scott, General Winfield, 167.
Sterling, A., 59 *n.*
Sheil, Richard, 66.
Simeon, Mr., 131.
Smith, Horace, 62.
Smith, the Misses, 62, 65 *n.*, 73.
Spa, Thackeray at, 15 *et seq.*
Sortain, Mr., 34.
Sutro, Dr., 22.

TAYLOR, Henry, 136, 156.
  Tennent, Lady, 53.
Thackeray, William Makepeace, circumstances of his correspondence with Mr. and Mrs. Brookfield, 1, 2; his visit to the Royal Scots Fusiliers in garrison, 10; his hour in Canterbury Cathedral, 11–13; journey to Brussels, 13; on Becky Sharp and others of his characters, 14; journey to Spa, 15 *et seq.*; on Titmarsh's reception at the Hôtel d'York, 16; in the play-house at Spa, 18, 19; his notes in verse, 25, 26; comments on "Pendennis," 29; writes for the *Chronicle*, 29; at Oxford and Blenheim, 31; on the service in Magdalen Chapel, 32; on Charles Buller's death, 33; on "blasphemous asceticism," 35; at Dover, 37; in Paris, 38; his "quarantine of family dinners," etc., 38; description of a French play, 39; on his work and money affairs, 43, 44; on Blanche Amory and Pendennis, 49; at the Reform banquet, 53; on "David Copperfield," 54; at Spencer Cowper's dinner, 56; at Brighton, 61; on his work on "Pendennis," 65, 67; on Dickens, 68; on old friendships, 70; in Paris again, 74; visits Jules Janin, 74; on his artist life in Paris, 77; on a rumor of his death, 81; his poem, "A Failure," 82; his fear of loss of memory, 84; in a French green-room, 88; his Christmas letter, 95; on his work, 97, 98; on a ride and the characters met in it, 102; in Paris again, 104, on d'Orsay, 111; at a French ball, 114; at Cambridge, 117; his "smash" at the Literary Fund, 120; on a visit to an emigrant ship, 124; his review of Fielding in the *Times*, 125; on handwritings, 129; on funerals, 129; his ode for the Exhibition, 132 *et seq.*; on the exhibition, 134; on mysticism, 139; on the Rhine, 143; at Wiesbaden, 144; at Heidelberg, 144; at Berne, 147; on his fortieth birthday, 147; at Lucerne, 149; in Paris again, 151; on the death of Mr. Brookfield's father, 157; in New York, 158; his lectures there, 160; in Philadelphia, 162; in Baltimore and Washington, 165; his opinion of American cities, 165; on his lectures, 168; at Richmond, 168; at Savannah, 169; on the *Saturday Review's* criticisms, 170; his imaginary letter from New York, 172; his resignation from *Punch*, 174; anecdotes of, 176 *et seq.*
Thackeray, Dr., 118.

Tidy, Mrs., 46.
Trench, Richard Chenevix, 155.
Turpin, Mrs. Brookfield's maid, 23, 93.

"VANITY FAIR," the *Spectator's* notice of, 10, 29 *n.*, 178 *et seq.*

Villiers, Charles, 100, 103.

WALDEGRAVE, Lady, 107.
Washington, Thackeray at, 165.
Whitmore, Mrs., 73.
Wiesbaden, Thackeray at, 144.
Wilmot, Foley, 153.

www.ingramcontent.com/pod-product-compliance
Lightning Source LLC
Chambersburg PA
CBHW020805230426
43666CB00007B/857